PAMPHILIA TO AMPHILANTHVS

by
Lady Mary Wroth

and

SALMACIS AND HERMAPHRODITVS

by
Francis Beaumont

PAMPHILIA
TO
AMPHILANTHVS

Lady Mary Wroth

The text of this edition follows that of the Mariott and Grismand printing of 1621.

PAMPHILIA

TO

AMPHILANTHVS

1.

When night's blacke Mantle could most darknesse proue,
And sleepe (deaths Image) did my senses hyre,
From Knowledge of my selfe, then thoughts did moue
Swifter then those, most swiftnesse neede require.
In sleepe, a Chariot drawne by wing'd Desire,
I saw; where sate bright *Venus* Queene of Loue,
And at her feete her Sonne, still adding Fire
To burning hearts, which she did hold aboue,
But one heart flaming more then all the rest,
The Goddesse held, and put it to my breast,
Deare Sonne now shoot, said she: thus must we winne;
He her obey'd, and martyr'd my poore heart.
I waking hop'd as dreames it would depart,
Yet since, O me, a Lover I haue beene.

2.

Deare eyes how well indeed, you doe adorne
That blessed Sphere, which gazing soules hold deare?
The loved place of sought for triumphs, neere
The Court of Glory, where Loues force was borne.
How may they terme you *Aprills* sweetest morne?
When pleasing lookes, from those bright lights appeare
A Sunne-shine day, from clowdes, and mists still cleare:
Kinde nursing fires for wishes yet vnborne.
Two Starres of Heauen sent downe to grace the Earth,
Plac'd in that Throne which gives all ioyes their birthe,
Shining, and burning; pleasing yet their Charmes:
Which wounding, euen in hurts are deem'd delights;
So pleasant is their force, so great their mights,
As happy they can tryumph in their harmes.

3.

Yet is there hope, then Love but play thy part,
Remember well thy selfe, and think on me;
Shine in those eyes which conquer'd haue my heart,
And see if mine, be slacke to answer thee.
Lodge in that breast, and pitty moouing see,
For flames which in mine burne in truest smart,
Exciling thoughts, that touch Inconstancy,
Or those which waste not in the constant Art,
Watch but my sleepe, if I take any rest,
For thought of you, my spirit so distrest,
As, pale and famish'd, I for mercy cry.
Will you your seruant leave: thinke but on this,
Who weares Love's Crowne, must not doe so amisse
But seeke their good, who on thy force do lye.

4.

Forbeare darke night, my ioyes now budd againe,
Lately growne dead, while cold aspects, did chill
The roote at heart, and my chiefe hope quite kill,
And thunders strooke me in my pleasures waine.
Then I alas with bitter sobs, and paine,
Priuately groan'd, my Fortunes present ill;
All light of comfort dimb'd, woes in prides fill,
With strange encrease of griefe, I grieu'd in vaine.
And most, when as a memory to good
Molested me, which still as witnes stood,
Of those best dayes, in former time I knew:
Late gone as wonders past, like the great Snow,
Melted and wasted, with what, change must know:
Now backe the life comes where as once it grew.

5.

Can pleasing sight, misfortune euer bring?
Can firme desire a painefull torment trye?
Can winning eyes proue to the heart a sting?
Or can sweet lips in Treason hidden lye?
The Sunne most pleasing, blindes the strongest eye,
If two much look'd on, breaking the sights string;
Desires still crost must unto mischiefe hie,
And as Despaire, a lucklesse chance may fling.
Eyes hauing won, reiecting proues a sting
Killing the budd before the tree doth spring;
Sweet lipps, not louing, doe as poyson proue:
Desire, sight, Eyes, lipps; seeke, see, proue, and finde,
You loue may winn, but curses if vnkinde,
Then show you harmes dislike, and ioy in loue.

6.

O striue not still to heape disdaine on me,
Nor pleasure take, your cruelty to show
On haplesse me, on whom all sorrowes flow,
And byding make: as giuen, and lost by thee.
Alas; eu'ne griefe is growne to pitty me,
Scorne cryes out 'gainst it selfe such ill to show,
And would giue place for ioyes delights to flow;
Yet wretched I, all tortures beare from thee.
Long haue I suffer'd, and esteem'd it deare,
Since such thy will, yet grew my paine more neere:
Wish you my end, say so, you shall it haue;
For all the deapth of my heart-held despaire,
Is that for you, I feele not Death for care,
But now Ile seeke it, since you will not saue.

Song 1.

The spring now come at last
To Trees, Fields, to Flowres,
And meadowes makes to taste
His pride, while sad showres
Which from mine eyes doe flow
Makes knowne with cruell paines,
Cold Winter yet remaines,
No signe of Spring we knowe.

The Sunne which to the Earth
Giues heate, light, and pleasure,
Ioyes in Spring, hateth Dearth,
Plenty makes his Treasure.
His heate to me is colde,
His light all darknesse is,
Since I am barrd of blisse,
I heate, nor light behold

A Shepherdesse thus said,
Who was with griefe opprest,
For truest Loue betrayd,
Barrd her from quiett rest:
And weeping thus, said shee,
My end approacheth neere,
Now Willow must I weare,
My fortune so will bee.

With Branches of this tree
Ile dresse my haplesse head,
Which shall my wittnes bee,
My hopes in Loue are dead:
My cloathes imbroder'd all,
Shall be with Garlands round,
Some scatter'd, others bound;
Some tyde, some like to fall.

The Barke my Booke shall bee,
Where dayly I will write,
This tale of haples mee,
True slaue to Fortunes spite.
The roote shall be my bedd,
Where nightly I will lye
Wailing inconstancy,
Since all true loue is dead.

And these Lines I will leaue,
If some such Louer come,
Who may them right conceiue,
and place them on my Tombe:
She who still constant lou'd
Now dead with cruell care,
Kill'd with unkind Dispaire,
And change, her end heere prou'd.

14

7.

Loue leaue to vrge, thou knowest thou hast the hand
'Tis Cowardize to striue where none resist,
Pray thee leaue off, I yeeld vnto thy band,
Doe not thus, still in thine owne power persist.
Behold, I yeeld; let forces be dismist,
I am thy Subiect conquer'd bound to stand
Neuer thy foe, but did thy claime assist,
Seeking thy due of those who did withstand.
But now it seemes thou would'st I should thee loue,
I doe confesse, t'was thy will made mee choose,
And thy faire shewes made me a Louer proue,
When I my freedome did for paine refuse.
Yet this Sir god, your Boy-ship I despise,
Your charmes I obey, but loue not want of eyes.

8.

Ledd by the power of griefe to wailings brought,
By false conceit of change fallen on my part;
I seeke for some smale ease by lines which bought,
Increase the paine; griefe is not cur'd by Art.
Ah! how vnkindnesse moues within the heart,
Which still is true and free from changing thought:
What vnknowne woe it breeds, what endlesse smart,
With ceaslesse teares which causelessly are wrought.
It makes me now to shun all shining light,
And seeke for blackest clouds me light to giue:
Which to all others only darkness driue;
They on me shine, for Sunne disdaines my sight.
Yet though I darke do liue, I triumph may,
Vnkindnes, nor this wrong shall loue allay.

9.

Be you all pleas'd, your pleasures grieue not me;
Doe you delight? I enuy not your ioy:
Haue you content? contentment with you be;
Hope you for blisse? Hope still, and still enioy.
Let sad misfortune, haplesse me destroy,
Leaue crosses to rule me, and still rule free:
While all delights their contraries imploy,
To keepe good backe, and I but torments see.
Ioyes are bereau'd me, harmes doe only tarry,
Despaire takes place, disdaine hath gott the hand:
Yet firme loue holds my senses in such band,
As (since dispis'ed) I with sorrow marry.
Then if with griefe I now must coupled bee,
Sorrow Ile wed; Despaire thus gouernes mee.

10.

The weary Traueller, who tyred, sought
In places distant farre, yet found no end
Of paine or labour, nor his state to mend:
At last with ioy is to his home backe brought.
Findes not more ease though he with ioy be fraught,
When past is feare content like soules ascend:
Then I, on whom new pleasures doe descend,
Which now as high as first-borne blisse is wrought.
He tyred with his paines, I with my minde;
He all content receiues by ease of lymbs:
I, greatest happinessse that I doe finde,
Beliefe for faith, while hope in pleasure swimmes.
Truth saith 'twas wrong conceit bred my despigt,
Which once acknowledg'd, brings my hearts delight.

11.

You endlesse torments that my rest opresse,
How long will you delight in my sad paine?
Will neuer Loue your fauour more expresse?
Shall I still liue, and euer feele disdaine?
Alasse now stay, and let my griefe obtaine
Some end; feede not my heart with sharpe distresse:
Let me once see my cruell fortunes gaine,
At least release, and long-felt woes redresse.
Let not the blame of cruelty disgrace
The honor'd title of your god-head Loue;
Giue not iust cause for me to say, a place
Is found for rage alone on me to moue.
O quickly end, and doe not long debate
My needful ayd, lest helpe doe come too late.

12.

Cloy'd with the torments of a tedious night,
I wish for day; which come, I hope for ioy:
When crosse I finde, new tortures to destroy,
My woe-kil'd heart, first hurt by mischiefs might.
Then crye for night, and once more day takes flight.
And brightnesse gone; what rest should heere inioy
Vsurped is: Hate will her force imploy;
Night cannot Griefe intombe though blacke as spite.
My thoughts are sad, her face as sad doth seeme;
My paines are long, Her howers tedious are;
My griefe is great, and endlesse is my care;
Her face, her force, and all of woes esteeme.
Then welcome Night, and farwell flattering Day,
Which all hopes breed, and yet our ioyes delay.

Song 2.

Aɫɫ *Night I weepe, all Day I cry, Ay me,*
I still doe wish, though yet deny, ay me;
I sigh, I mourne, I say that still,
I only am the store for ill, ay me.

In coldest hopes I freeze, yet burne, ay me,
From flames I striue to fly, yet turne, ay me:
From griefe I hast, but sorrowes hye,
And on my heart all woes do lye, ay me.

From contraries I seeke to run, ay me,
But contraries I cannot shun, ay me:
For they delight their force to trye,
And to Despaire my thoughts doe ty, ay me.

Whither alasse then shall I goe, ay me,
When as Despaire all hopes outgoe, ay me:
If to the Forrest Cupid hies,
And my poore soule to his law tyes, ay me.

To the Court: O no. He cryes fye, ay me,
There no true loue you shall espy, ay me:
Leaue that place to falsest Louers,
Your true loue all truth discouers, ay me,
Then quiet rest, and no more proue, ay me,
All places are alike to Loue, ay me:
And constant be in this begun,
Yet say, till Life with Loue be dunn Ay me.

13.

Deare famish not what you your selfe gaue food,
Destroy not what your glory is to saue:
Kill not that soule to which you spirit gaue,
In pitty, not disdaine, your triumph stood.
An easie thing it is to shed the bloud
Of one who at your will yeelds to the graue:
But more you may true worth by mercy craue,
When you preserue, not spoyle, but nourish good.
Your sight is all the food I doe desire,
Then sacrifice me not in hidden fire,
Or stop the breath which did your praises moue.
Think but how easie 'tis a sight to giue,
Nay euen desert, since by it I doe liue,
I but Camelion-like, would liue, and loue.

14.

Am I thus conquer'd? haue I lost the powers,
That to withstand, which ioyes to ruine me?
Must I bee still, while it my strength deuoures,
And captiue leads me prisoner bound, vnfree?
Loue first shall leaue mens phant'sies to them free,
Desire shall quench loues flames, Spring, hate sweet showres;
Loue shall loose all his Darts, haue sight, and see
His shame and wishings, hinder happy houres.
Why should we not loues purblinde charmes resist?
Must we be seruile, doing what he list?
No, seeke some hoste too harbour thee: I flye
Thy babish tricks, and freedome doe professe;
But O my hurt makes my lost heart confesse:
I loue, and must; so farewell liberty.

15.

Truly (poore night) thou welcome art to me,
I loue thee better in this sad attire
Then that which rayseth some mens fant'sies higher,
Like painted outsides, which foule inward be.
I loue thy graue and saddest lookes to see,
Which seems my soule and dying heart entire,
Like to the ashes of some happy fire,
That flam'd in ioy, but quench'd in misery.
I loue thy count'nance, and thy sober pace,
Which euenly goes, and as of louing grace
To vs, and mee among the rest opprest,
Giues quiet peace to my poore selfe alone,
And freely grants day leaue; when thou art gone,
To giue cleare light, to see all ill redrest.

16.

Sleepe fye possesse me not, nor doe not fright
Me with thy heauy, and thy deathlike might:
For counterfetting's vilder then death's sight;
And such deluding more my thoughts doe spight.
Thou suffer'st falsest shapes my soule t'affright,
Sometimes in likenesse of a hopefull spright;
And oft times like my Loue, as in despight;
Ioying, thou canst with malice kill delight.
When I (a poore foole made by thee) thinke ioy
Doth flow, when thy fond shadowes doe destroy
My that while sencelesse selfe, left free to thee.
But now doe well, let me for euer sleepe,
And so for euer that deere Image keepe
Or still wake that my senses may be free.

17.

Sweet shades, why doe you seeke to giue delight
To me, who deeme delight in this vilde place:
But torment, sorrow, and mine owne disgrace,
To taste of ioy, or your vaine pleasing sight?
Show them your pleasures who saw neuer night
Of griefe, where ioyings fawning smiling face
Appears as day, where griefe found neuer space:
Yet for a sigh, a groane, or enuies spite.
But O: on me a world of woes doe lye,
Or els on me all harmes striue to relye,
And to attend like seruants bound to me.
Heate in desire, while frosts of care I proue,
Wanting my loue, yet surfet doe with loue,
Burne, and yet freeze, better in Hell to be.

18.

Which should I better like of, day or night?
Since all the day, I liue in bitter woe:
Inioying light more cleere my wrongs to know,
And yet most sad, feeling in it all spite;
In night when darknesse doth forbid all light;
Yet see I griefe apparant to the show,
Follow'd by iealousie, whose fond tricks flow,
And on vnconstant waues of doubt alight.
I can behold rage cowardly to feede
Vpon foule error, which these humors breede,
Shame doubt and feare, yet boldly will thinke ill.
All those in both I feele, then which is best
Darke to ioy by day, light in night opprest?
Leaue both and end, these but each other spill.

Song 3.

Stay my thoughts do not aspire,
To vaine hopes of high desire;
See you not all meanes bereft,
To inioye no ioye is left,
Yet still me thinkes my thoughts doe say,
Some hopes do liue amid dismay.

Hope then once more, hope for ioy,
Bury feare which ioyes destroy,
Thought hath yet some comfort giuen,
Which despaire hath from vs driuen:
Therefore deerely my thoughts cherish,
Neuer let such thinking perish.

'Tis an idle thing to plaine,
Odder farre to dye for paine;
Thinke and see how thoughts doe rise,
Winning where there noe hope lies;
Which alone is louers treasure,
For by thoughts we loue doe measure.

Then kinde thought my fant'sie guide,
Let me neuer haplesse slide;
Still maintaine thy force in me,
Let me thinking still be free;
Nor leaue thy might vntill my death,
But let me thinking yeeld vp breath.

19.

Come darkest Night, becomming sorrow best,
Light leaue thy light, fit for a lightsome soule:
Darknesse doth truely sute with me opprest,
Whom absence power doth from mirthe controule.
The very trees with hanging heads condole
Sweet Summers parting, and of leaues distrest,
In dying colours make a grief-full role;
So much (alas) to sorrow are they prest.
Thus of dead leaues, her farewell carpets made,
Their fall, their branches, all their mournings proue,
With leaulesse naked bodies, whose hues vade
From hopefull greene to wither in their loue.
If trees, and leaues for absence mourners be,
No maruell that I grieue, who like want see.

20.

The Sunne which glads, the earth at his bright sight,
When in the morne he showes his golden face,
And takes the place from tedious drowsie Night.
Making the world still happy in his grace.
Shewes happinesse remaines not in one place,
Nor may the Heauens alone to vs giue light,
But hide that cheerfull face, though noe long space,
Yet long enough for tryall of their might.
But neuer Sun-set could be so obscure,
No Desart euer had a shade so sad:
Nor could black darknesse euer proue so bad,
As paines which absence makes me now indure.
The missing of the Sunne awhile makes Night,
But absence of my ioy sees neuer light.

21.

When last I saw thee, I did not thee see,
It was thine Image which in my thoughts lay
So liuely figur'd, as no times delay
Could suffer me in heart to parted be.
And sleepe so fauourable is to me,
As not to let thy lou'd remembrance stray:
Lest that I waking might haue cause to say,
there was one minute found to forgett thee.
Then, since my faith is such, so kinde my sleepe,
That gladly thee presents into my thought,
And still true Louer-like thy face doth keepe,
So as some pleasure shadow-like is wrought.
Pitty my louing, nay of consience giue
Reward to me in whom thy self doth liue.

22.

Like to the Indians scorched with the Sunne,
The Sunne which they doe as their God adore:
So am I vs'd by Loue, for euermore
I worship him, lesse fauors haue I wonne.
Better are they who thus to blacknesse run,
And so can onely whitenesse want deplore:
Then I who pale and white am with griefes store,
Nor can haue hope, but to see hopes vndone.
Beesides their sacrifice receiu'd in sight,
Of their chose Saint, mine hid as worthlesse rite,
Grant me to see where I my offerings giue.
Then let me weare the marke of *Cupids* might,
In heart, as they in skin of *Phoebus* light,
Not ceasing offerings to Loue while I Liue.

23.

When euery one to pleasing pastime hies
Some hunt, some hauke, some play, while some delight
In sweet discourse, and musicke shewes ioys might:
Yet I my thoughts doe farr aboue these prize.
The ioy which I take is, that free from eyes
I sit and wonder at this day-like night,
So to dispose themselues as voyd of right,
And leaue true pleasure for poore vanities.
When others hunt, my thoughts I haue in chase;
If hauke, my minde at wished end doth flye:
Discourse, I with my spirit talke and cry;
While others musicke choose as greatest grace.
O God say I, can thes fond pleasures moue,
Or musicke bee but in sweet thoughts of Loue?

24.

Once did I heare an aged father say
Vnto his sonne, who with attention heares
What Age and wise experience euer cleares
From doubts of feare, or reason to betray.
My Sonn (said hee) behold thy father gray,
I once had as thou hast, fresh tender yeares,
And like thee sported destitute of feares;
But my young faults made me too soone decay.
Loue once I did, and like thee, fear'd my Loue,
Led by the hatefull thread of Ielousie,
Striuing to keepe, I lost my liberty,
And gain'd my griefe, which still my sorrowes moue.
In time shun this, to loue is no offence,
But doubt in Youth, in Age, breeds penitence.

Song 4.

Sweetest *Loue returne againe,*
Make not too long stay;
Killing mirth and forcing paine;
Sorrow leading way:
Let vs not thus parted be,
Loue, and absence nere agree.

But since you must needs depart,
And me haplesse leaue;
In your iourney take my heart,
Which will not deceiue:
Yours it is, to you it flies,
Ioying in those loued eyes.

So in part we shall not part,
Though we absent be,
Tyme, nor place, nor greatest smart,
Shall my bands make free:
Tyed I am, yet thinke it gaine,
In such knots I feele no paine.

But can I liue, hauing lost
Chiefest part of me?
Heart is fled, and sight is crost,
These my fortunes be:
Yet deare heart goe, soone returne,
As good there as heere to burne.

25.

Poore eyes bee blinde, the light behold noe more,
Since that is gon which is your deare delight:
Rauish'd from you by greater powre, and might,
Making your losse a gaine to others store.
Oerflow and drowne, till sight to you restore
That blessed Starre, and as in hatefull spight,
Send forth your teares in flouds to kill all sight,
And looks, that lost wherin you ioy'd before.
Bury these beames which in some kindled fires,
And conquer'd haue their loue-burnt hearts desires,
Losing, and yet no gaine by you esteem'd;
Till that bright Starre doe once againe appeare,
Brighter then *Mars* when hee doth shine most cleare;
See not then by his might be you redeem'd.

26.

Deare cherish this, and with it my soules will,
Nor for it ran away doe it abuse:
Alas it left (poore me) your brest to choose,
As the blest shrine, where it would harbour still.
Then fauour shew, and not vnkindly kill
The heart which fled to you, but doe excuse
That which for better did the wurse refuse;
And pleas'd Ile be, though heartlesse my lyfe spill.
But if you will bee kinde, and iust indeed,
Send me your heart, which in mine's place shall feede
On faithfull loue to your deuotion bound,
There shall it see the sacrifices made
Of pure and spottlesse Loue, which shall not vade,
While soule, and body are together found.

27.

Fie tedious Hope, why doe you still rebell?
Is it not yet enough you flatter'd me,
But cuningly you seeke to vse a Spell
How to betray; must these your Trophies bee?
I look'd from you farre sweeter fruite to see,
But blasted were your blossomes when they fell:
And those delights expected from hands free,
Wither'd and dead, and what seemd blisse proues hell.
No Towne was won by a more plotted slight
Then I by you, who may my fortune write,
In embers of that fire which ruin'd me:
Thus Hope your falshood calls you to be tryde,
You'r loth, I see, the tryall to abide;
Proue true at last, and gaine your liberty.

28.

Griefe, killing griefe, haue not my torments beene
Already great and strong enough? but still
Thou dost increase, nay glory in mine il,
And woes new past, afresh new woes begin?
Am I the onely purchase thou canst win?
Was I ordain'd to giue despaire her fill,
Or fittest I should mount misfortunes hill,
Who in the plaine of ioy cannot liue in?
If it be so, Griefe come as welcome guest,
Since I must suffer for anothers rest;
Yet this (good Griefe) let me intreat of thee,
Vse still thy force, but not from those I loue
Let me all paines and lasting torments proue;
So I misse these, lay all thy waights on me.

29.

Fly hence O! Ioy, noe longer heere abide,
Too great thy pleasures are for my despaire
To looke on, losses now must proue my fare;
Who not long since on better foode relide.
But foole, how oft had I Heau'ns changing spi'de
Before of mine owne fate I could haue care:
Yet now past time, I can too late beware,
When nothings left but sorrowes faster ty'de.
While I inioyd that Sunne, whose sight did lend
Me ioy, I thought that day could haue no end:
But soon a night came cloath'd in absence darke;
Absence more sad, more bitter then is gall,
Or death, when on true Louers it doth fall;
Whose fires of loue, disdaine reasts poorer sparke.

30.

You blessed shades, which giue me silent rest,
Witnes but this when death hath clos'd mine eyes,
And separated me from earthly tyes;
Being from hence to higher places adrest.
How oft in you I haue laine heere opprest?
And haue my miseries in wofull cryes
Deliuer'd forth, mounting vp to the Skyes?
Yet helplesse, backe return'd to wound my brest,
Which wounds did but striue how to breed more harm
To me, who can be cur'd by no one charme
But that of Loue, which yet may me releeue;
If not, let Death my former paines redeeme,
My trusty friends, my faith vntouch'd, esteeme,
And witnesse I could loue, who so could grieue.

Song 5.

Time only cause of my vnrest,
By whom I hop'd once to be blest,
How cruell art thou turn'd?
That first gau'st lyfe vnto my loue,
And still a pleasure not to moue,
Or change, though euer burn'd.

Haue I thee slack'd, or left vndone
One louing rite, and so haue wonne,
Thy rage, or bitter changing?
That now noe minutes I shall see,
Wherein I may least happy be,
Thy fauours so estranging.

Blame thy selfe, and not my folly,
Time gaue time but to be holy,
True Loue, such ends best loueth:
Unworthy Loue doth seeke for ends,
A worthy Loue but worth pretends;
Nor other thoughts it proueth.

Then stay thy swiftnes cruell Time,
And let me once more blessed clime
To ioy, that I may prayse thee:
Let me pleasure sweetly tasting,
Ioy in Loue, and faith not wasting,
and on Fames wings Ile raise thee.

Neuer shall thy glory dying,
Be vntill thine owne vntying,
That Tyme noe longer liueth,
'Tis a gaine such time to lend,
Since so thy fame shall neuer end,
But ioy for what she giueth.

31.

After long trouble in a tedious way,
Of Loues vnrest, laid downe to ease my paine,
Hoping for rest, new torments I did gaine
Possessing me, as if I ought t'obey.
When Fortune came, though blinded, yet did stay,
And in her blessed armes did me inchaine:
I, cold with griefe, thought noe warmth to obtaine,
Or to dissolue that yce of ioyes decay.
Till rise (said she) Reward to thee doth send
By me the seruant of true Louers, ioy:
Bannish all clouds of doubt, all feares destroy;
And now on Fortune, and on Loue depend.
I her obey'd, and rising felt that Loue
Indeed was best, when I did least it moue.

32.

How fast thou fliest, O time, on loues swift wings,
To hopes of ioy, that flatters our desire:
Which to a Louer still contentment brings;
Yet when we should inioy, thou dost retire.
Thou stay'st thy pace (faulse Time) from our desire
When to our ill thou hast'st with Eagles wings:
Slow only to make vs see thy retire
Was for Despaire, and harme, which sorrowe brings.
O! slake thy pace, and milder passe to Loue,
Be like the Bee, whose wings she doth but vse
To bring home profit; masters good to proue,
Laden, and weary, yet againe pursues.
So lade thy selfe with hony of sweet ioy,
And do not me the Hiue of Loue destroy.

33.

How many eyes (poore Loue) hast thou to guard
Thee from thy most desired wish, and end?
Is it because some say thou'rt blinde, that barr'd
From sight, thou should'st noe happinesse attend?
Who blame thee soe, smale iustice can pretend,
Since twixt thee and the Sunne no question hard
Can be, his sight but outward, thou canst bend
The heart, and guide it freely thus vnbar'd.
Art thou, while we both blinde and bold, oft dare
Accuse the of the harmes, our selues should finde:
Who led with folly, and by rashnesse blinde
Thy sacred power doe with a child's compare.
Yet Loue, this boldnesse pardon; for admire
Thee sure we must, or be borne without fire.

34.

Take heed mine eyes, how you your looks doe cast,
Lest they betray my hearts most secret thought:
Be true vnto your selues; for nothing's bought
More deare then Doubt, which brings a Louers fast.
Catch you al watching eyes ere they be past,
Or take yours fix't, where your best Loue hath sought
The pride of your desires; let them be taught
Their faults for shame they could no truer last.
Then looke, and looke with ioy, for conquest won,
Of those that search'd your hurt in double kinde:
So you kept safe, let them themselues looke blinde,
Watch, gaze, and marke till they to madnesse run.
While you mine eyes enioye full sight of Loue,
Contented that such happinesses moue.

35.

False hope which feeds but to destroy, and spill
What it first breeds, vnnaturall to the birth
Of thine owne wombe, conceiuing but to kill
And plenty giues to make the greater dearth.
So Tyrants doe, who falsly ruling Earth,
Outwardly grace them, and with profits fill,
Aduance those who appointed are to death;
To make their greater fall to please their will.
Thus shadow they their wicked vile intent,
Colouring euill with a show of good:
While in faire showes their malice so is spent;
Hope kill's the heart, and Tyrants shed the blood.
For Hope deluding brings vs to the pride
Of our desires the farther downe to slide.

36.

How well (poore heart) thou witnesse canst, I loue,
How oft my grief hath made thee shed forth teares,
Drops of thy dearest blood; and how oft feares
Borne testimony of the paines I proue?
What torments hast thou suffer'd, while aboue
Ioy thou tortur'd wert with racks, which longing beares:
Pinch'd with desires, which yet but wishing reares
Firme in my faith, in constancie, to moue.
Yet is it said, that sure loue cannot be,
Where so small shew of passion is descri'd:
When thy chiefe paine is, that I must it hide
From all, saue onely one, who should it see.
For know, more passion in my heart doth moue,
Then in a million that make shew of loue.

Song 6.

Y*ou happy blessed eyes,*
Which in that ruling place,
Haue force both to delight, and to disgrace;
Whose light allures and tyes
All hearts to your command:
O looke on me, who doe at mercy stand.

'Tis you that rule my life,
T'is you my comforts giue,
Then let not scorne to me my ending driue:
Nor let the frownes of strife
Haue might to hurt those lights;
Which while they shine they are true loues delights.

See but when Night appeares,
And Sunne hath lost his force,
How his loss doth all ioye from vs diuorce:
And when he shines, and cleares
The Heauens from clowdes of Night,
How happy then is made our gazing sight?

But more then Sun's faire light
Your beames doe seeme to me,
Whose sweetest lookes doe tye, and yet make free:
Why should you then so spight
Poore me? as to destroy
The only pleasure that I taste of ioy?

Shine then, O dearest lights
With fauour and with loue
And let no cause, your cause of frownings moue:
But as the soules delights,
So blesse my then blesst eyes,
Which vnto you their true affection tyes.

Then shall the Sunne giue place,
As to your greater might,
Yeelding that you doe show more perfect light.
O then but grant this grace,
Unto your Loue-tide slaue,
To shine on me, who to you all faith gaue.

And when you please to frowne,
Vse your most killing eyes
On them, who in vntruth and falsehood lies,
But (Deare) on me cast downe
Sweet lookes, for true desire;
That banish doe all thoughts of faigned fire.

37.

Night, welcome art thou to my minde distrest,
Darke, heauy, sad, yet not more sad then I:
Neuer could'st thou find fitter company
For thine owne humour, then I thus opprest.
If thou beest darke, my wrongs still vnredrest
Saw neuer light, nor smallest blisse can spye:
If heauy ioy from me too fast doth hie,
And care out-goes my hope of quiet rest.
Then now in friendship ioyne with haplesse me,
Who am as sad and darke as thou canst be,
Hating all pleasure or delight of lyfe,
Silence, and griefe, with thee I best doe loue.
And from you three I know I can not moue,
Then let vs liue companions without strife.

38.

What pleasure can a banish'd creature haue
In all the pastimes that inuented are
By wit or learning? Absence making warre
Against all peace that may a biding craue.
Can wee delight but in a welcome graue,
Where we may bury paines? and so be fare
From loathed company, who alwaies iarre
Vpon the string of mirth that pastime gaue.
The knowing part of ioye is deem'd the heart,
If that be gone what ioy can ioy impart
When senceless is the feeler of our mirth?
Noe, I am banish'd, and no good shall finde,
But all my fortunes must with mischiefe binde;
Who but for miserie did gaine a birth.

39.

If I were giuen to mirth, 'twould be more crosse,
Thus to be robbed of my chiefest ioy:
But silently I beare my greatest losse
Who's vs'd to sorrow, griefe will not destroy.
Nor can I as those pleasant wits inioy
Mine owne fram'd wordes, which I account the drosse
Of purer thoughts, or reckon them as mosse,
While they (wit-sick) themselues to breath imploy.
Alas, thinke I, your plenty shewes your want;
For where most feeling is, wordes are more scant,
Yet pardon mee, liue, and your pleasure take.
Grudge not if I (neglected) enuy show,
'Tis not to you that I dislike doe owe;
But (crost my self) wish some like me to make.

40.

It is not Loue which you poore fooles do deeme,
That doth appeare by fond and outward showes
Of kissing, toying, or by swearings gloze:
O no, these are farre off from loues esteeme.
Alas, they are not such that can redeeme
Loue lost, or wining keepe those chosen blowes:
Though oft with face, and lookes loue ouerthrowes;
Yet so slight conquest doth not him beseeme.
'Tis not a shew of sighes or teares can proue
Who loues indeed, which blasts of fained loue,
Increase or dye, as fauors from them slide.
But in the soule true loue in safety lies
Guarded by faith, which to desert still hies:
And yet kinde lookes doe many blessings hide.

41.

You blessed Starres, which doe Heauen's glory show,
And at your brightnesse make our eyes admire:
Yet enuy not, though I on earth below,
Inioy a sight which moues in me more fire.
I doe confesse such beauty breeds desire
You shine, and clearest light on vs bestow:
Yet doth a sight on Earth more warmth inspire
Into my louing soule, his grace to know.
Cleare, bright, and shining, as you are, is this
Light of my ioy: fix't stedfast, nor will moue
His light from me, nor I chang from his loue;
But still increase as th'eith of all my blisse.
His sight giues life vnto my loue-rould eyes,
My loue content, because in his loue lies.

42.

If euer loue had force in humane brest,
If euer he could moue in pensiue heart:
Or if that he such powre could but impart
To breed those flames, whose heat brings ioys vnrest.
Then looke on me; I am to these adrest,
I am the soule that feeles the greatest smart:
I am that heartlesse Trunck of hearts depart;
And I that One, by loue, and griefe opprest
Non euer felt the truth of loues great misse
Of eyes till I depriued was of blisse;
For had he seene, he must haue pitty show'd.
I should not haue beene made this Stage of woe,
Where sad Disasters haue their open show:
O no, more pitty he had sure bestow'd.

Song 7.

Sorrow, *I yeeld, and grieue that I did misse;*
Will not thy rage be satified with this?
As sad a Diuell as thee,
Made me vnhappy be:
Wilt thou not yet consent to leaue, but still
Striue how to show thy cursed diuelish skill?

I mourne, and dying am, what would you more?
My soule attends, to leaue this cursed shoare
Where harmes doe only flow,
Which teach me but to know
The saddest houres of my lifes vnrest,
And tyred minutes with griefes hand opprest.

Yet all this will not pacifie thy spight,
No, nothing can bring ease but my last night,
Then quickly let it be,
While I vnhappy see
That time so sparing, to grant Louers blisse,
Will see for time lost, there shall no griefe misse.

Nor let me euer cease from lasting griefe,
But endlesse let it be without reliefe;
To winn againe of Loue,
The fauour I did prooue,
And with my end please him, since dying, I
Haue him offended, yet vnwillingly.

43.

O dearest eyes, the lights, and guides of Loue,
The ioyes of *Cupid*, who himselfe borne blinde,
To your bright shining, doth his tryumphs binde;
For, in your seeing doth his glory moue.
How happy are those places where you prooue
Your heauenly beames, which make the Sun to finde
Enuy and grudging, he so long hath shin'd
For your cleare lights, to match his beames aboue.
But now alas, your sight is heere forbid,
And darkenes must these poore lost roomes possesse,
So be all blessed lights from henceforth hid,
That this blacke deede of darknesse haue excesse.
For why showld Heauen affoord least light to those,
Who for my misery such darkenesse chose.

44.

How fast thou hast'st O Spring with sweetest speede
To catch thy waters which before are runne,
And of the greater Riuers welcome woone,
Ere these thy new-borne streames these places feed.
Yet you doe well, lest staying here might breede
Dangerous flouds, your sweetest bankes t'orerunn,
And yet much better my distresse to shunn,
Which maks my tears your swiftest course succeed.
But best you doe when with so hasty flight
You fly my ills, which now my selfe outgoe,
Whose broken heart can testifie such woe,
That so orecharg'd, my life-bloud, wasteth quite.
Sweet Spring then keepe your way be neuer spent,
And my ill dayes, or griefes, assunder rent.

45.

Good now be still, and doe not me torment,
With multituds of questions, be at rest,
And onely let me quarrell with my breast,
Which stil lets in new stormes my soule to rent.
Fye, will you still my mischiefes more augment?
You saye, I answere crosse, I that confest
Long since, yet must I euer be opprest,
With your tongue torture which will ne're be spent?
Well then I see no way but this will fright,
That Deuill speech; alas, I am possest,
And madd folks senseles are of wisdomes right,
The hellish spirit, Absence, doth arrest.
All my poore senses to his cruell might,
Spare me then till I am my selfe, and blest.

46.

Loue thou hast all, for now thou hast me made
So thine, as if for thee I were ordain'd,
Then take thy conquest, nor let me be pain'd
More in thy Sunne, when I doe seeke thy shade.
No place for helpe haue I left to inuade,
That shew'd a face where least ease might be gain'd;
Yet found I paine increase, and but obtain'd,
That this no way was to haue loue allay'd
When hott, and thirsty, to a Well I came,
Trusting by that to quench part of my flame,
But there I was by Loue afresh imbrac'd
Drinke I could not, but in it I did see
My selfe a liuing glasse as well as shee;
For loue to see himselfe in, truely plac'd.

47.

O stay mine eyes shed not these fruitlesse teares,
Since hope is past to win you back againe,
That treasure which being lost breeds all your paine;
Cease from this poore betraying of your feares.
Thinke this too childish is, for where griefe reares
So high a powre for such a wretched gaine:
Sighes nor laments should thus be spent in vaine,
True sorrow neuer outward wailing beares.
Be rul'd by me, keepe all the rest in store,
Till no roome is that may containe one more;
Then in that Sea of teares, drowne haplesse me,
And Ile prouide such store of sighes, as part
Shall be enough to breake the strongest heart,
This done, we shall from torments freed be.

48.

How like a fire doth loue increase in me!
The longer that it lasts the stronger still;
The greater, purer, brighter; and doth fill
No eye with wonder more then hopes still bee.
Bred in my breast, when fires of Loue are free
To vse that part to their best pleasing will,
And now vnpossible it is to kill
The heate so great where Loue his strength doth see.
Mine eyes can scarce sustaine the flames, my heart
Doth trust in them my passions to impart,
And languishingly striue to shew my loue.
My breath not able is to breathe least part
Of that increasing fuell of my smart;
Yet loue I will, till I but ashes proue.
Pamphilia.

49

Let griefe as farre be from your dearest breast
As I doe wish, or in my hands to ease;
Then should it banish'd be, and sweetest rest
Be plac'd to giue content by Loue to please.
Let those disdaines which on your heart do seaze,
Doubly returne to bring her soules vnrest:
Since true loue will not that belou'd displease;
Or let least smart to their minds be addrest.
But oftentimes mistakings be in loue.
Be they as farre from false accusing right,
And still truth gouerne with a constant might
So shall you only wished pleasures proue.
And as for mee she that shewes you least scorne,
With all despite and hate, be her heart torne.

Song 8

O *me, the time is come to part,*
And with it my life-killing smart:
Fond Hope leaue me, my deare must goe,
To meete more ioy, and I more woe.

Where still of mirth inioy thy fill,
One is enough to suffer ill:
My heart so well to sorrow vs'd,
can better be by new griefes bruis'd.

Thou whom the Heauens themselues like made,
should neuer sit in mourning shade:
No, I alone must mourne and end,
Who haue a life in griefe to spend.

My swiftest pace to wailings bent,
Shewes ioy had but a short time lent,
To bide in me where woes must dwell,
And charme me with their cruell spell.

And yet when they their witchcrafts trye,
They only make me wish to dye:
But ere my faith in loue they change,
In horrid darknesse will I range.

Song 9

S*ay* Venus *how long haue I lou'd, and seru'd you heere?*
Yet all my passions scorn'd or doubted, although cleere;
Alas thinke loue deserueth loue, and you haue lou'd,
Looke on my paines, and see if you the like haue prou'd:
Remember then you are the Goddesse of Desire,
and that your sacred powre hath touch'd and felt this fire.

Perswade these flames in me to cease, or them redresse
In me (poore me) who stormes of loue haue in excesse,
My restlesse nights may show for me, how much I loue,
My sighes vnfaignd can witnes what my heart doth proue:
My saddest lookes doe show the griefe my soule indures,
Yet all these torments from your hands no helpe procures.

Command that wayward Child your Son to grant your right,
and that his Bow and shafts he yeeld to your faire sight,
To you who haue the eyes of ioy, the heart of loue,
And then new hopes may spring, that I may pitty moue:
Let him not triumph that he can both hurt and saue,
And more, bragge that to you your self a wound he gaue.

Rule him, or what shall I expect of good to see?
Since he that hurt you, he (alas) may murther mee.

Song 10

I *that am of all most crost,*
Hauing, and that had haue lost,
May with reason thus complaine,
Since loue breeds loue, and loues paine.

That which I did most desire,
To allay my louing fire,
I may haue, yet now must misse,
Since another Ruler is.

Would that I no Ruler had,
Or the seruice not so bad,
Then might I with blis enioy
That which now my hopes destroy.

And that wicked pleasure got,
Brings with it the sweetest lot:
I that must not taste the best,
Fed, must starue, and restlesse rest.

Song 11

Loue as well can make abiding
In a faithfull Shepheards brest
As in Princes: whose thoughts sliding
Like swift riuers neuer rest.

Change to their minds is best feeding,
To a sheapheard all his care,
Who when his loue is exceeding,
Thinks his faith his richest fare.

Beauty but a slight inuiting,
Cannot stirre his heart to change;
Constancye his chiefe delighting,
Striues to flee from fant'sies strange,

Fairnesse to him is no pleasure,
If in other then his loue;
Nor can esteeme that a treasure,
Which in her smiles doth not moue.

This a shepheard once confessed,
Who lou'd well, but was not lou'd:
Though with scorne & griefe oppressed
could not yet to change be mou'd.

But himselfe he thus contented,
While in loue he was accurst:
This hard hap he not repented,
Since best Louers speed the worst.

Song 12

Dearest if I by my deseruing,
May maintaine in your thoughts my loue,
Let me it still enioy;
Nor faith destroy:
Butt pitty Loue where it doth moue.

Let no other new Loue inuite you,
To leaue me who so long haue serud:
Nor let your power decline
But purely shine
On me, who haue all truth preseru'd.

Or had you once found my heart straying,
Then would not I accuse your change,
But being constant still
It needs must kill
One whose soule knowes not how to range.

Yet may you Loues sweet smiles recouer,
Since all loue is not yet quite lost,
But tempt not Loue too long
Lest so great wrong
Make him thinke he is too much crost.

Song 13

Fairest *and still truest eyes,*
Can you the lights be, and the spies
Of my desires?
Can you shine cleare for loues delight,
And yet the breeders be of spight,
And iealous fires?

Mark what lookes doe you behold,
Such as by Iealousie are told
They want your Loue.
See how they sparckle in distrust,
Which by a heate of thoughts vniust
In them doe mooue.

Learne to guide your course by Art,
Change your eyes into your heart,
And patient be:
Till fruitlesse Ielousie giue leaue,
By safest absence to receiue
What you would see.

Then let Loue his triumph haue,
And Suspition such a graue,
As not to mooue.
While wished freedome brings that blisse
That you enioy what all ioy is
Happy to Loue.

Sonnet. 1.

In night yet may we see some kinde of light,
When as the Moone doth please to shew her face,
And in the Sunns roome yeelds her light, and grace,
Which otherwise must suffer dullest night:
So are my fortunes barrd from true delight,
Cold, and vncertaine, like to this strange place,
Decreasing, changing in an instant space,
And euen at full of ioy turnd to despight.
Iustly on Fortune was bestowd the Wheele,
Whose fauours fickle, and vnconstant reele,
Drunke with delight of change and sudden paine;
Where pleasure hath no setled place of stay,
But turning still, for our best hopes decay,
And this (alas) we louers often gaine.

2.

Loue like a Iugler, comes to play his prize,
And all mindes draw his wonders to admire,
To see how cunningly he (wanting eyes)
Can yet deseiue the best sight of desire.
The wanton Childe, how he can faine his fire
So prettily, as none sees his disguise,
How finely doe his trickes; while we fooles hire
The badge, and office of his tyrannies.
For in the ende such Iugling he doth make,
As he our hearts instead of eyes doth take;
For men can onely by their slights abuse,
The sight with nimble, and delightfull skill,
But if he play, his gaine is our lost will,
Yet Child-like we cannot his sports refuse.

3.

Most blessed night, the happy time for Loue,
The shade for Louers, and their Loues delight,
The raigne of Loue for seruants free from spight,
The hopefull seasons, for ioyes sports to mooue.
Now hast thou made thy glory higher prooue,
Then did the God, whose pleasant Reede did smite
All *Argus* eyes into a death-like night,
Till they were safe, that none could Loue reprooue.
Now thou hast cloas'd those eyes from prying sight
That nourish Iealousie, more than ioyes right,
While vaine Suspition fosters their mistrust,
Making sweet sleepe to master all suspect,
Which els their priuat feares would not neglect,
But would embrace both blinded, and vniust.

4.

Cruell suspition, O! be now at rest,
Let daily torments bring to thee some stay,
Alas, make not my ill thy ease-full pray,
Nor giue loose raines to Rage, when Loue's opprest.
I am by care sufficiently distrest,
No Racke can stretch my heart more, nor a way
Can I find out, for least content to lay
One happy foot of ioy, one step that's blest.
But to my end thou fly'st with greedy eye,
Seeking to bring griefe by bace Iealousie;
O, in how strange a Cage am I kept in?
No little signe of fauour can I prooue,
But must be way'd, and turn'd to wronging loue,
And with each humour must my state begin.

5.

How many nights haue I with paine endurd?
Which as so many Ages I esteem'd,
Since my misfortune, yet noe whit redeem'd
But rather faster ty'de, to griefe assur'd.
How many houres haue my sad thoughts endur'd
Of killing paines? yet is it not esteem'd
By cruell Loue, who might haue these redeemd,
And all these yeeres of houres to ioy assur'd.
But fond Childe, had he had a care to saue,
As first to conquer, this my pleasures graue,
Had not beene now to testifie my woe.
I might haue beene an Image of delight,
As now a Tombe for sad misfortunes spight,
Which Loue vnkindly, for reward doth show.

6.

My paine still smother'd in my grieued brest,
Seekes for some ease, yet cannot passage finde,
To be discharg'd of this vnwellcome guest,
When most I striue, more fast his burthens binde.
Like to a Ship on *Goodwins* cast by winde,
The more she striues, more deepe in Sand is prest,
Till she be lost: so am I in this kind
Sunck, and deuour'd, and swallow'ed by vnrest.
Lost, shipwrackt, spoyl'd, debar'd of smallest hope,
Nothing of pleasure left, saue thoughts haue scope,
Which wander may; goe then my thoughts and cry:
Hope's perish'd, Loue tempest-beaten, Ioy lost,
Killing Despaire hath all these blessings crost;
Yet Faith still cries, Loue will not falsifie.

7.

An end fond Ielousie, alas I know
Thy hiddenest, and thy most secret Art,
Thou canst no new inuention frame but part,
I haue already seene, and felt with woe.
All thy dissemblings, which by faigned showe,
Wonne my beliefe, while truth did rule my heart,
I with glad minde embrac'd, and deemd my smart
The spring of ioy, whose streames with blisse should flow.
I thought excuses had beene reasons true,
And that no falshood could of thee ensue,
So soone beliefe in honest mindes is wrought;
But now I finde thy flattery, and skill,
Which idely made me to obserue thy will,
Thus is my learning by my bondage bought.

8.

Poore Loue in chaines, and fetters like a thiefe
I mett ledd forth, as chast *Diana's* gaine
Vowing the vntaught Lad should no reliefe
From her receiue, who gloried in fond paine.
She call'd him theife; with vowes he did mainetaine
He neuer stole, but some sadd slight of griefe
Had giuen to those who did his power disdaine,
In which reuenge, his honour was the chiefe.
Shee say'd he murther'd and therefor must dye,
He that he caus'd but Loue, did harmes deny,
But, while she thus discoursing with him stood;
The Nymphes vnti'de him, and his chaines tooke off,
Thinking him safe; but he (loose) made a scoffe,
Smiling and scorning them; flew to the wood.

9.

Pray doe not vse these words, I must be gone;
Alasse doe not foretell mine ills to come:
Let not my care be to my ioyes a Tombe;
But rather finde my losse with losse alone.
Cause me not thus a more distressed one,
Not feeling blisse, because of this sad doome
Of present crosse; for thinking will orecome
And loose all pleasure, since griefe breedeth none.
Let the misfortune come at once to me,
Nor suffer me with griefe to punish'd be;
Let mee be ignorant of mine owne ill:
Then now with the fore-knowledge quite to lose
That which with so much care and paines Loue chose
For his reward, but ioye now, then mirth kill.

10.

Folly would needs make me a Louer be,
When I did litle thinke of louing thought;
Or euer to be tyde, while shee told me
That none can liue, but to these bands are brought.
I (ignorant) did grant, and so was bought,
And sold againe to Louers slauery:
The duty to that vanity once taught,
Such band is, as wee will not seeke to free.
Yet when I well did vnderstand his might,
How he inflam'd, and forc'd one to affect:
I loud and smarted, counting it delight
So still to waste, which Reason did reiect.
When Loue came blind-fold, and did challenge me.
Indeed I lou'd, but wanton Boy not hee,

Song 14

The *Spring time of my first louing,*
Finds yet no winter of remouing;
Nor frosts to make my hopes decrease:
But with the Summer still increase.

The trees may teach vs Loue's remaining,
Who suffer change with little paining,
Though Winter make their leaues decrease,
Yet with the Summer they increase.

As birds by silence show their mourning
in colde, yet sing at Springs returning:
So may Loue nipt awhile decrease,
but as the Summer soone increase.

Those that doe loue but for a season,
Doe faulsifie both Loue and Reason:
For Reason wills, if Loue decrease,
It like the Summer should increase.

Though Love sometimes may be mistaken,
the truth yet ought not to be shaken:
Or though the heate awhile decrease,
It with the Summer may increase.

And since the Spring time of my louing
Found neuer Winter of remouing:
Nor frosts to make my hopes decrease,
Shall as the Summer still increase.

Song 15

Loue a childe is euer crying,
Please him, and he strait is flying;
Giue him, he the more is crauing,
Neuer satisfi'd with hauing.
His desires haue no measure,
Endlesse folly is his treasure:
What he promiseth, he breaketh,
Trust not one word that he speaketh.
Hee vowes nothing but false matter,
And to cousen you hee'l flatter:
Let him gain the hand, hee'l leaue you,
And still glory to deceiue you.

Hee will triumph in your wailing,
And yet cause be of your failing:
these his vertues are, and slighter
are his guifts, his fauours lighter.

Feathers are as firme in staying,
Wolues no fiercer in their praying.
As a child then leaue him crying,
Nor seeke him so giu'n to flying.

BEeing past the paines of loue,
Freedome gladly seekes to moue:
Sayes that Loues delights were pretty;
But to dwell in them t'were pitty,

And yet truly sayes, that Loue
Must of force in all hearts moue:
But though his delights are pretty,
To dwell on them were a pitty.

Let Loue slightly passe like Loue,
Neuer let it too deepe moue:
For though Loues delights are pretty,
To dwell in them were great pitty.

Loue no pitty hath of Loue,
Rather griefes then pleasures moue:
So though his delights are pretty,
To dwell in them would be pitty.

Those that like the smart of Love,
In them let it freely move:
Els though his delights are pretty,
Doe not dwell in them for pitty

O pardon *Cupid*, I confesse my fault,
Then mercy grant me in so iust a kinde:
For treason neuer lodged in my minde
Against thy might, so much as in a thought.
And now my folly I haue dearely bought,
Nor could my soule least rest or quiett finde;
Since Rashnes did my thoughts to Error binde,
Which now thy fury, and my harme hath wrought.
I curse that thought, and hand which that first fram'd,
For which by thee I am most iustly blam'd:
But now that hand shall guided be aright,
And giue a Crowne vnto thy endlesse praise,
Which shall thy glory, and thy greatnesse raise,
More then these poore things could thy honor spight.

A Crowne of Sonnet dedicated to LOVE.

In this strange Labyrinth how shall I turne,
Wayes are on all sids while the way I misse:
If to the right hand, there, in loue I burne,
Let mee goe forward, therein danger is.
If to the left, suspition hinders blisse;
Let mee turne back, shame cryes I ought returne:
Nor faint, though crosses with my fortunes kiss,
Stand still is harder, allthough sure to mourne.
Thus let mee take the right, or left hand way,
Goe forward, or stand still, or back retire:
I must these doubts indure without allay
Or helpe, but trauell finde for my best hire.
Yet that which most my troubled sense doth moue,
Is to leaue all, and take the threed of Loue.

2.

Is to leaue all, and take the threed of Loue,
Which line straite leades vnto the soules content,
Where choice delights with pleasures wings doe moue,
And idle fant'sie neuer roome had lent.
When chaste thoughts guide vs, then our minds are bent
To take that good which ills from vs remoue:
Light of true loue brings fruite which none repent;
But constant Louers seeke and wish to proue.
Loue is the shining Starre of blessings light,
The feruent fire of zeale, the roote of peace,
The lasting lampe, fed with the oyle of right,
Image of Faith, and wombe for ioyes increase.
Loue is true Vertue, and his ends delight,
His flames are ioyes, his bands true Louers might.

3.

His flames are ioyes, his bandes true Louers might,
No stain is there, but pure, as purest white,
Where no cloud can appaere to dimme his light,
Nor spot defile, but shame will soon requite.
Heere are affections, tryde by Loues iust might
As Gold by fire, and black discern'd by white;
Error by truth, and darknes knowne by light,
Where Faith is vallu'd, for Loue to requite.
Please him, and serue him, glory in his might
And firme hee'le be, as Innocency white,
Cleere as th'ayre, warme as Sun's beames, as day light
Iust as Truth, constant as Fate, ioy'd to requite.
Then loue obey, striue to obserue his might
And be in his braue Court a glorious light.

4.

And be in his braue Court a glorious light
Shine in the eyes of Faith, and Constancy
Maintaine the fires of Loue, still burning bright,
Not slightly sparkling, but light flaming be.
Neuer to slake till earth no Starres can see,
Till Sun, and Moone doe leaue to vs darke night,
And secound Chaos once againe doe free
Vs, and the World from all deuisions spight,
Till then affections which his followers are,
Gouerne our hearts, and prooue his powers gaine,
To taste this pleasing sting, seeke with all care
For happy smarting is it with small paine.
Such as although it pierce your tender heart,
And burne, yet burning you will loue the smart.

5.

And burne, yet burning you will loue the smart,
When you shall feele the waight of true desire,
So pleasing, as you would not wish your part
Of burthen showld be missing from that fire.
But faithfull and vnfaigned heate aspire
Which sinne abollisheth, and doth impart
Salues to all feare, with vertues which inspire
Soules with diuine loue; which showes his chast art.
And guide he is to ioyings, open eyes
He hath to happinesse, and best can learne
Vs, meanes how to deserue, this he descries,
Who blinde, yet doth our hiden'st thoughts discerne.
Thus we may gaine since liuing in blest Loue,
He may our profitt, and our Tutor prooue.

6.

He may our Prophett, and our Tutor prooue,
In whom alone we doe this power finde,
To ioine two hearts as in one frame to mooue
Two bodies, but one soule to rule the minde
Eyes which must care to one deare Obiect binde,
Eares to each others speach as if aboue
All else, they sweete, and learned were; this kind
Content of Louers witnesseth true loue.
It doth inrich the wits, and make you see
That in your selfe which you knew not before,
Forceing you to admire such guifts showld be
Hid from your knowledge, yet in you the store.
Millions of these adorne the throane of Loue,
How blest be they then, who his fauours proue?

7.

How bless'd be they, then, who his fauors proue,
A life whereof the birth is iust desire?
Breeding sweete flame, which harts inuite to moue,
In these lou'd eyes which kindle *Cupids* fire,
And nurse his longings with his thoughts intire,
Fix't on the heat of wishes form'd by Loue,
Yet whereas fire destroyes, this doth aspire,
Increase, and foster all delights aboue.
Loue will a Painter make you, such, as you
Shall able be to draw, your onely deare,
More liuely, perfect, lasting, and more true
Then rarest Workeman, and to you more neere.
These be the least, then all must needs confesse,
He that shuns Loue, doth loue himselfe the lesse.

8.

He that shuns Loue, doth loue himselfe the lesse,
And cursed he whose spirit, not admires
The worth of Loue, where endlesse blessednes
Raignes, & commands, maintain'd by heau'nly fires.
Made of Vertue, ioyn'd by Truth, blowne by Desires,
Strengthned by Worth, renew'd by carefulnesse,
Flaming in neuer changing thoughts: bryers
Of Iealousie shall heere misse welcomnesse.
Nor coldly passe in the pursutes of Loue
Like one long frozen in a Sea of yce:
And yet but chastly let your passions mooue,
No thought from vertuous Loue your minds intice.
Neuer to other ends your Phant'sies place,
But where they may returne with honor's grace.

9.

But where they may returne with Honor's grace,
Where *Venus* follies can no harbour winne,
But chased are, as worthlesse of the face,
Or stile of Loue, who hath lasciuious beene.
Our hearts are subiect to her Sonne; where sinne
Neuer did dwell, or rest one minutes space;
What faults he hath in her did still beginne,
And from her breast he suck'd his fleeting pace.
If Lust be counted Loue 'tis falsely nam'd,
By wickednesse, a fairer glosse to set
Vpon that Vice, which else makes men asham'd
In the owne Phrase to warrant, but beget
This Childe for Loue, who ought like Monster borne
Be from the Court of Loue, and Reason torne.

10.

Be from the Court of Loue, and Reason torne,
For Loue in Reason now doth put his trust,
Desert, and liking are together borne
Children of Loue, and Reason, Parents iust,
Reason aduiser is, Loue ruler must
Be of the State, which Crowne he long hath worne;
Yet so, as neither will in least mistrust
The gouernment where no feare is of scorn.
Then reuerence both their mights thus made of one,
But wantonesse, and all those errors shun,
Which wrongers be, Impostures, and alone
Maintainers of all follies ill begunne.
Fruit of a sowre, and vnwholsome grownd
Vnprofitably pleasing, and vnsound.

11.

Vnprofitably pleasing, and vnsound.
When Heauen gaue liberty to fraile dull earth,
To bringe foorth plenty that in ills abound,
Which ripest, yet doe bring a certaine dearth.
A timelesse, and vnseasonable birth,
Planted in ill, in worse time springing found,
Which Hemlocke like might feed a sicke-wits mirth
Where vnrul'd vapours swimme in endlesse round.
Then ioy we not in what we ought to shunne,
Where shady pleasures shew, but true borne fires
Are quite quench'd out, or by poore ashes won,
Awhile to keepe those coole, and wann desires.
O no, let Loue his glory haue, and might
Be giu'n to him, who triumphs in his right.

12.

Be giu'n to him who triumphs in his right;
Nor fading be, but like those blossomes faire,
Which fall for good, and lose their colours bright,
Yet dye not, but with fruit their losse repaire:
So may Loue make you pale with louing care,
When sweet enioying shall restore that light,
More cleere in beauty, then we can compare,
If not to *Venus* in her chosen night.
And who so giue themselues in this deare kinde,
These happinesses shall attend them still,
To be supplide with ioyes enrich'd in minde,
With treasures of content, and pleasures fill.
Thus loue to be deuine, doth here appeare,
Free from all foggs, but shining faire, and cleare.

13.

Free from all foggs, but shining faire, and cleare,
Wise in all good, and innocent in ill,
Where holly friendship is esteemed deare,
With Truth in loue, and Iustice in our Will.
In Loue these titles onely haue their fill
Of happy life-maintainer, and the meere
Defence of right, the punisher of skill,
And fraude, from whence directions doth appeare.
To thee then, Lord commander of all hearts,
Ruler of our affections, kinde, and iust,
Great King of Loue, my soule from faigned smarts,
Or thought of change, I offer to your trust,
This Crowne, my selfe, and all that I haue more,
Except my heart, which you bestow'd before.

14.

Except my heart, which you bestow'd before,
And for a signe of Conquest gaue away
As worthlesse to be kept in your choice store;
Yet one more spotlesse with you doth not stay.
The tribute which my heart doth truely pay,
Is faith vntouch'd, pure thoughts discharge the score
Of debts for me, where Constancy beares sway,
And rules as Lord, vnharm'd by Enuies sore,
Yet other mischiefes faile not to attend,
As enimies to you, my foes must be,
Curst Iealousie doth all her forces bend
To my vndoing, thus my harmes I see.
So though in Loue I feruently doe burne,
In this strange Labyrinth how shall I turne?

Song 1

Sweet, *let me enioy thy sight*
More cleare, more bright then morning Sun,
Which in Spring-time giues delight
And by which Summers pride is wun.
Present sight doth pleasures moue
Which in sad absence we must misse:
But when met againe in loue,
Then twice redoubled is our blisse.

Yet this comfort absence giues,
And only faithfull louing tries,
That though parted, Loues force liues
As iust in heart, as in our eyes:
But such comfort banish quite,
Farre sweeter is it, still to finde
Fauour in thy loued sight,
Which present smiles with ioyes combind.

Eyes of gladnesse, lipps of Loue,
And hearts from passion not to turne,
But in sweet affections mooue,
In flames of Faith to liue, and burne.
Dearest then, this kindnesse giue,
And grant me life, which is your sight,
Wherein I more blessed liue,
Then graced with the Sunnes faire light.

2.

Sweet Siluia in a shady wood,
With her faire Nimphs layd downe,
Saw not farre off where Cupid stood,
The Monarch of Loues Crowne,
All naked, playing with his wings,
Within a Mirtle Tree,
Which sight a sudden laughter brings,
His Godhead so to see.

And fondly they began to iest,
With scoffing, and delight,
Not knowing he did breed vnrest,
And that his will's his right:
When he perseiuing of their scorne,
Grew in such desperate rage,
Who but for honour first was borne,
Could not his rage asswage.

Till shooting of his murth'ring dart,
Which not long lighting was
Knowing the next way to the heart,
Did through a poore Nymph passe:
This shot the others made to bow,
Besides all those to blame,
Who scorners be, or not allow
Of powerfull Cupids name.

Take heede then nor doe idly smile,
Nor Loues commands despise,
For soone will he your strength beguile,
Although he want his eyes.

3.

Come merry Spring delight vs,
For Winter long did spight vs,
In pleasure still perseuer,
Thy beauties ending neuer:
Spring, and grow
Lasting so,
With ioyes increasing euer.

Let cold from hence be banish'd,
Till hopes from me be vanish'd,
But blesse thy daynties growing
In fulnesse freely flowing:
Sweet Birds sing
For the Spring,
All mirth is now bestowing.

Philomel in this Arbour
Makes now her louing Harbour,
Yet of her state complaining,
Her Notes in mildnesse strayning,
Which thought sweet,
Yet doe meet.
Her former lucklesse paining.

4.

Louers learne to speake but truth,
Sweare not, and your oathes forgoe,
Giue your age a constant youth,
Vow noe more then what you'le doe.

Thinke it sacriledge to breake
What you promise, shall in loue
And in teares what you doe speake
Forget not, when the ends you proue.

Doe not thinke it glory is
To entice, and then deceiue,
Your chiefe honors lye in this,
By worth what wonne is, not to leaue.

'Tis not for your fame to try,
What we weake, not oft refuse,
In our bounty our faults lye,
When you to doe a fault will chuse.

Fye leaue this, a greater gaine,
tis to keepe when you haue won,
Then what purchas'd is with paine,
Soone after in all scorne to shun.

For if worthlesse to be priz'd,
Why at first will you it moue?
And if worthy, why dispis'd?
You cannot sweare, and lie, and loue.

Loue alasse you cannot like,
Tis but for a fashion mou'd,
None can chuse, and then dislike,
Vnlesse it be by faslhood prou'd.

But your choyce is, and your loue.
How most number to deceiue,
As if honors claime did moue
Like Popish Lawe, none safe to leaue.

Flye this folly, and returne
Vnto truth in Loue, and try,
None but Martir's happy burne,
More shamefull ends they haue that lye.

1.

My heart is lost, what can I now expect,
An euening faire after a drowsie day?
Alas, fond Phant'sie, this is not the way,
To cure a mourning heart, or salue neglect:
They who should helpe, doe me, and helpe reiect,
Embracing loose desires, and wanton play,
While wanton base delights doe beare the sway,
And impudency raignes without respect.
O *Cupid* let thy Mother know her shame,
'T'is time for her to leaue this youthfull flame,
Which doth dishonor her, is ages blame,
And takes away the greatnes of thy name.
Thou God of Loue, she only Queene of lust,
Yet striues by weakning thee, to be vniust.

2.

Late in the Forrest I did *Cupid* see
Cold, wett, and crying, he had lost his way,
And being blinde was farther like to stray;
Which sight, a kind compassion bred in me.
I kindly tooke, and dry'd him, while that he,
(Poore Child) complain'd, he sterued was with stay
And pin'd for want of his accustom'd prey,
For none in that wilde place his Host would be.
I glad was of his finding, thinking sure,
This seruice should my freedome still procure,
And in my armes I tooke him then vnharm'd,
Carrying him safe vnto a Myrtle bowre,
But in the way he made me, feele his powre,
Burning my heart, who had him kindly warm'd.

3.

I*vno* still iealous of her husband *Ioue*,
Descended from aboue, on earth to try,
Whether she there could find his chosen Loue,
Which made him from the Heau'ns so often flye.
Close by the place where I for shade did lye,
She chaseing came, but when shee saw me moue,
Haue you not seene this way (said she) to hye
One, in whom vertue neuer grownde did proue?
Hee, in whom Loue doth breed, to stirre more hate,
Courting a wanton Nimph for his delight;
His name is *Iupiter*, my Lord, by Fate,
Who for her, leaues Me, Heauen, his Throne, and light,
I saw him not (said I) although heere are
Many, in whose hearts, Loue hath made like warre.

4.

When I beheld the Image of my deare,
With greedy lookes mine eies would that way bend,
Feare, and Desire, did inwardly contend;
Feare to be mark'd, Desire to drawe still neere.
And in my soule a Spirit would appeare,
Which boldnes waranted, and did pretend
To be my *Genius*, yet I durst not lend,
My eyes in trust, where others seem'd so cleare.
Then did I search, from whence this danger rose,
If such vnworthynesse in me did rest,
As my steru'd eyes must not with sight be blest,
When Iealousie her poyson did disclose.
Yet in my heart vnseene of Iealous eye,
The truer Image shall in tryumph lye.

5.

Like to huge Clowdes of smoake which well may hide
The face of fairest day, though for a while:
So wrong may shaddow me, till truth doe smile,
And Iustice Sunne-like hath those vapours tyde.
O doating Time, canst thou for shame let slid,
So many minutes, while ills doe beguile
Thy age, and worth, and falshoods thus defile
Thy auncient good, where now but crosses bide?
Looke but once vp, and leaue thy toyling pace
And on my miseries thy dimme eye place,
Goe not so fast, but giue my care some ende,
Turne not thy glasse (alas) vnto my ill
Since thou with sand it canst not so farre fill,
But to each one my sorrowes will extend.

6.

O that no day would euer more appeare,
But clowdy night to gouerne this sad place,
Nor light from Heauen these haples roomes to grace
Since that light's shadow'd which my Loue holds deare.
Let thickest mists in enuy master here,
And Sunne-borne day for malice show no face,
Disdaining light, where *Cupid*, and the race
Of Louers are dispisd, and shame shines cleere.
Let me be darke, since barr'd of my chiefe light,
And wounding Iealousie commands by might,
But stage-play-like diguised pleasures giue:
To me it seemes, as ancient fictions make
The Starres, all fashions, and all shapes partake,
While in my thoughts true forme of Loue shall liue.

7.

No time, no roome, no thought, or writing can
Giue rest, or quiet to my louing heart,
Or can my memory or Phant'sie scan,
The measure of my still renewing smart.
Yet whould I not (deare Loue) thou shouldst depart,
But let my passions as they first began,
Rule, wounde, and please, it is thy choysest Art,
To giue disquiet, which seemes ease to man.
When all alone, I thinke vpon thy paine,
How thou doest trauell our best selues to gaine,
Then houerly thy lessons I doe learne;
Thinke on thy glory, which shall still ascend,
Vntill the world come to a finall end,
And then shall we thy lasting powre dicerne.

8.

How Glowworme-like the Sun doth now appeare,
Cold beames doe from his glorious face descend
Which shewes his daies, and force draw to an end,
Or that to leaue taking, his time grows neere.
This day his face did seeme but pale, though cleare,
The reason is, he to the North must lend
His light, and warmth must to that Climat bend,
Whose frozen parts cowld not loues heat hold deare
Alas, if thou bright Sunne to part from hence
Grieue so, what must I haplesse who from thence,
Where thou dost goe my blessing shall attend;
Thou shalt enioy that sight for which I dye,
And in my heart thy fortunes doe enuy,
Yet grieue, I'le loue thee, for this state may mend.

9.

My Muse now happy lay thy selfe to rest,
Sleepe in the quiet of a faithfull loue,
Write you no more, but let these Phant'sies mooue
Some other hearts, wake not to new vnrest.
But if you Study be those thoughts adrest
To truth, which shall eternall goodnes prooue;
Enioying of true ioy the most, and best
The endles gaine which neuer will remoue.
Leaue the discourse of *Venus*, and her sonne
To young beginners, and their braines inspire
With storyes of great Loue, and from that fire,
Get heat to write the fortunes they haue wonne.
And thus leaue off; what's past shewes you can loue,
Now let your Constancy your Honor proue.

FINIS.

SALMACIS

AND

HERMAPHRODITVS

Salmacida spolia sine sanguine
& sudore.

Francis Beaumont

The text is from the 1602 edition in the Bodleian Library.

To the True Patronesse of all Poetrie,
CALIOPE

IT is a statute in deepe wisdomes lore,
That for his lines none should a patron chuse
By wealth or pouerty, by lesse or more,
But who the same is able to peruse;
Nor ought a man his labours dedicate,
	Without a true and sensible desert,
To any power of such a mighty state,
And such a wise Defendresse as thou art.
Thou great and powerfull Muse, then pardon mee,
That I presume the Mayden-cheeke to stayne,
In dedicating such a work to thee,
Sprung from the issue of an idle brayne.
	I vse thee as a woman ought to be:
	I consecrate my idle howres to thee.

In Laudem Authoris.

Like to the weake estate of a poore friend,
To whom sweet fortune hath bene euer slow,
Which dayly doth that happy howre attend,
When his poore state may his affection shew:
So fares my loue, not able as the rest,
To chaunt thy prayses in a lofty vayne,
Yet my poore Muse doth vow to doe her best,
And wanting wings, shee'le tread an humble strayne.
I thought at first her homely steps to rayse,
And for some blazing Epithites to looke,
But then I fear'd, that by such wondrous prayse,
Some men would grow suspicious of thy booke:
    For hee that doth thy due deserts reherse,
Depriues that glory from thy worthy verse.

W. B.

To the Author.

Eyther the goddesse drawes her troupe of loues
From Paphos, where she erst was held diuine,
And doth vnyoke her tender-necked Doues,
Placing her seat in this small papry shine;
Or the sweet Graces through th'Idalian groue,
Led the blest Author in their daunced rings;
Or wanton Nymphs in watry bowres haue woue,
With fine Mylesian threds, the verse he sings;
Or curious *Pallas* once again doth striue,
With prowd *Arachne* for illustrious glory,
And once againe doth loues of gods reuiue,
Spinning in silken twists a lasting story:
    If none of these, then *Venus* chose his sight,
    To leade the steps of her blind sonne aright.

I. B.

To the Author.

The matchlesse Lustre of faire poesie,
Which erst was bury'd in old Romes decayes,
Now'gins with height of rising maiesty,
Her dust-wrapt head from rotten tombes to rayse,
    And with fresh splendor gilds her topelesse crest,
    Rearing her palace in our Poets brest.

The wanton Ouid, whose inticing rimes
Haue with attractiue wonder forc't attention,
No more shall be adir'd at: for these times
Produce a Poet, whose more mouing passion
    Will teare the loue-sick mirtle from his browes,
    T'adorne his Temple with deserued bowes.

The strongest Marble feares the smallest rayne:
The rusting Canker eates the purest gold:
Honours best dye dreads enuies blackest stayne:
The crimson badge of beautie must waxe old.
    But this faire issue of thy fruitful brayne,
    Nor dreads age, enuie, cankring rust, or rayne.

A. F.

The Author to the Reader.

I sing the fortunes of a lucklesse payre,
Whose spotlesse soules now in one body be:
For beauty still is *Prodromus* to care,
Crost by the sad starres of natiuitie;
And of the strange inchauntment of a well
Gi'n by the gods my sportiue Muse doth write,
Which sweet-lipt *Ouid* long agoe did tell,
Wherein who bathes, strait turnes *Hermaphrodite*.
    I hope my Poeme is so liuely writ,
      That thou wilt turne halfe-mayd with reading it.

Salmacis and Hermaphroditus

MY wanton lines doe treate of amorous loue,
Such as would bow the hearts of gods aboue:
Then *Venus*, thou great Citherean Queene,
That hourely tript on the Idalian greene,
Thou laughing *Erycina*, daygne to see
The verses wholly consecrate to thee;
Temper them so within thy Paphian shrine,
That euery Louers eye may melt a line;
Commaund the god of Loue that little King,
To giue each verse a sleight touch with his wing,
That as I write, one line may draw the tother,
And euery word skip nimbly o're another.
There was a louely boy the Nymphs had kept,
That on the Idane mountains oft had slept,
Begot and borne by powers that dwelt aboue,
By learned *Mercury* of the Queene of loue:
A face he had that shew'd his parents fame,
And from them both conioynd, he drew his name:
So wondrous fayre he was that (as they say)
Diana being hunting on a day,
Shee saw the boy vpon a greene banke lay him,
And there the virgin-huntresse meant to slay him,
Because no Nymphes did now pursue the chase:
For all were strooke blind with the wanton's face.
But when that beauteous face *Diana* saw,

Her armes were nummed, & shee could not draw;
Yet she did striue to shoot, but all in vaine,
Shee bent her bow, and loos'd it streight againe.
Then she began to chide her wanton eye,
And fayne would shoot, but durst not see him die,
She turnd and shot, and did of purpose misse him,
Shee turnd againe, and did of purpose kisse him.
Then the boy ran: for (some say) had he stayd,
Diana had no longer bene a mayd.
Phoebus so doted on this rosiat face,
That he hath oft stole closely from his place,
When he did lie by fayre *Leucothoes* side,
To dally with him in the vales of Ide:
And euer since this louely boy did die,
Phoebus each day about the world doth flie,
And on the earth he seekes him all the day,
And euery night he seekes him in the sea:
His cheeke was sanguine, and his lip as red
As are the blushing leaues of the Rose spred:
And I haue heard, that till this boy was borne,
Rose grew white vpon the virgin thorne,
Till one day walking to a pleasant spring,
To heare how cunningly the birds could sing,
Laying him downe vpon a flowry bed,
The Roses blush'd and turn'd themselues to red.
The Rose that blush'd not, for his great offence,
The gods did punish, and for impudence
They gaue this doome that was agreed by all,
The smell of the white Rose should be but small.
His haire was bushie, but it was not long,
The Nymphs had done his tresses mighty wrong:
For as it grew, they puld away his haire,
And made abilliments of gold to weare.
His eyes were *Cupids*: for vntill his birth,

Cupid had eyes, and liu'd vpon the earth,
Till on a day, when the great Queene of loue
Was by her white doues drawn from heauen aboue,
Vnto the top of the Idalian hill,
To see how well the Nymphs their charge fulfill,
And whether they had done the goddesse right,
In nursing of her sweet *Hermaphrodite*:
Whom when she saw, although complete & full,
Yet she complaynd, his eyes were somewhat dull:
And therefore, more the wanton boy to grace,
She puld the sparkling eyes from *Cupids* face,
Fayning a cause to take away his sight,
Because the Ape would sometimes shoot for spight.
But *Venus* set those eyes in such a place,
As grac'd those cleare eyes with a clearer face.
For his white hand each goddesse did him woo:
For it was whiter then the driuen snow:
His legge was straighter then the thigh of *Ioue*:
And he farre fairer then the god of loue.
When first this wel-shapt boy, beauties chiefe king,
Had seene the labour of the fifteenth spring,
How curiously it paynted all the earth,
He 'gan to trauaile from his place of birth,
Leauing the stately hils where he was nurst,
And where the Nymphs had brought him vp at first:
He lou'd to trauaile to the coasts vnknowne,
To see the regions farre beyond his owne,
Seeking cleare watry springs to bathe him in:
(For he did loue to wash his iuory skinne)
The louely Nymphes haue oft times seene him swimme,
And closely stole his clothes from off the brim,
Because the wanton wenches would so fayne
See him come nak'd to ask his clothes againe.
He lou'd besides to see the Lycian grounds,

And know the wealthy Carians vtmost bounds.
Vsing to trauaile thus, one day he found
A cristall brook, that tril'd along the ground,
A brooke, that in reflection did surpasse
The cleare reflection of the clearest glasse.
About the side there grew no foggy reedes,
Nor was the fount compast with barren weedes:
But liuing turfe grew all along the side,
And grasse that euer flourisht in his pride.
Within this brook a beauteous Nymph did dwell,
Who for her comely feature did excell;
So faire she was, of such a pleasing grace,
So straight a body, and so sweet a face,
So soft a belly, such a lustie thigh,
So large a forehead, such a cristall eye,
So soft and moyst a hand, so smooth a brest,
So faire a cheeke, so well in all the rest,
That *Iupiter* would reuell in her bowre,
Were he to spend againe his golden showre:
Her teeth were whiter then the mornings milke,
Her lip was softer then the softest silke,
Her haire as farre surpast the burnisht gold,
As siluer doth excell the basest mold:
Ioue courted her for her translucent eye,
And told her, he would place her in the skye,
Promising her, if she would be his loue,
He would ingraue her in the heauen aboue,
Telling this louely Nymph, that if he would,
He could deceiue her in a showre of gold,
Or like a Swanne come to her naked bed,
And so deceiue her of her maiden-head:
But yet, because he thought that pleasure best,
Where each consenting ioynes each louing brest,
He would put off that all-commaunding crowne,

Whose terrour strooke th'aspiring Giants downe,
That glittereing crown, whose radiant sight did tosse
Great *Pelion* from the top of mighty Osse,
He would depose from his world-swaying head,
To taste the amorous pleasures of her bed:
This added he besides, the more to grace her,
Like a bright starre he would in heauens vault place her.
By this the proud lasciuious Nymph was mou'd,
Perceiuing by great *Ioue* shee was belou'd,
And hoping as a starre she should ere long,
Be sterne or gracious to the Sea-mans song,
(For mortals still are subiect to their eye,
And what it sees, they striue to get as hie:)
She was contented that almighty *Ioue*
Should haue the first and best fruits of her loue:
(For women may be likened to the yeere,
Whose first fruits still do make the dayntiest cheere)
But yet *Astræa* first should plight her troth,
For the performance of *Ioues* sacred oth.
(Iust times decline, and all good dayes are dead,
When heauenly othes had need be warranted)
This heard great *Iupiter* and lik'd it well,
And hastily he seeks *Astræas* cell,
About the massie earth searching her towre:
But she had long since left this earthly bowre,
And flew to heauen aboue, lothing to see
The sinfull actions of humanitie.
Which when *Ioue* did perceiue, he left the earth,
And flew vp to the place of his owne birth,
The burning heauenly throne, where he did spy
Astræas palace in the glittering skie.
This stately towre was builded vp on hie,
Farre from the reach of any mortall eye;
And from the palace side there did distill

A little water, through a little quill,
The dewe of iustice, which did seldome fall,
And when it dropt, the drops were very small.
Glad was great *Ioue* when he beheld her towre,
Meaning a while to rest him in her bowre;
And therefore sought to enter at her dore:
But there was such a busie rout before;
Some seruing men, and some promooters bee,
That he could passe no foote without a fee:
But as he goes, he reaches out his hands,
And payes each one in order as he stands;
And still, as he was paying those before,
Some slipt againe betwixt him and the dore.
At length (with much adoo) he past them all,
And entred straight into a spacious hall,
Full of dark angles, and of hidden wayes,
Crooked Maranders, infinite delays;
All which delayes and entries he must passe,
Ere he could come where iust *Astræa* was.
All these being past by his immortall wit,
Without her doore he sawe a porter sit,
An aged man, that long time there had beene,
Who vs'd to search all those that entred in,
And still to euery one he gaue this curse,
None must see Iustice but with emptie purse.
This man searcht *Ioue* for his owne priuate gaine,
To haue the money which did yet remaine,
Which was but small: for much was spent before
On the tumultuous rout that kept the dore.
When he had done, he broght him to the place
Where he should see diuine *Astræas* face.
Then the great King of gods and men in went,
And saw his daughter *Venus* there lament,
And crying lowd for iustice, whom *Ioue* found

Kneeling before *Astræa* on the ground,
And still she cry'd and beg'd for a iust doome
Against blacke *Vulcan*, that vnseemely groome,
Whome she had chosen for her onely loue,
Though she was daughter to great thundering *Ioue*:
And thought the fairest goddesse, yet content
To marrie him, though weake and impotent;
But for all this they alwayes were at strife:
For euermore he ralyd at her his wife,
Telling her still, Thou art no wife of mine,
Anothers strumpet, *Mars* his concubine.
By this *Astræa* spyde almighty *Ioue*,
And bow'd her finger to the Queene of loue,
To cease her sute, which she would hear anon,
When the great King of all the world was gone.
Then she descended from her stately throne,
Which seat was builded all of Iasper stone,
And o're the seat was paynted all aboue,
The wanton vnseene stealths of amorous *Ioue*;
There might a man behold the naked pride
Of louely *Venus* in the vales of Ide,
When *Pallas*, and *Ioues* beauteous wife and she
Stroue for the prise of beauties raritie:
And there lame *Vulcan* and his *Cyclops* stroue
To make the thunderbolts for mighty *Ioue*:
From this same stately throne she down descended,
And sayd, The griefs of *Ioue* should be amended,
Asking the King of gods what lucklesse cause,
What great contempt of states, what breach of lawes
(For sure she thought, some vncouth cause befell,
That made him visit poore *Astræas* cell)
Troubled his thought: and if she might decide it,
Who vext great, *Ioue*, he deareley should abide it.
Ioue onely thankt her, and beganne to show

His cause of comming (for each one doth know
The longing words of Louers are not many,
If they desire to be inioyd of any.
Telling *Astræa,* It might now befall,
That she might make him blest, that blesseth all:
For as he walk'd vpon the flowry earth,
To which his owne hands whilome gaue a birth,
To see how streight he held it and how iust
He rold this massy pondrous heape of dust,
He laid him downe by a coole riuer side,
Whose pleasant water did so gently slide
With such soft whispering: for the brook was deepe,
That it had lul'd him in a heauenly sleepe.
When first he laid him downe, there was none neere him:
(for he did call before, but none could heare him)
But a faire Nymph was bathing when he wak'd,
(Here sigh'd great *Ioue,* and after brought forth) nak'd,
He seeing lou'd, the Nymph yet here did rest,
Where iust *Astræa* might make *Ioue* be blest,
If she would passe her faithfull word so farre,
As that great *Ioue* should make the mayd a starre.
Astræa yeelded: at which *Ioue* was pleas'd,
And all his longing hopes and feares were eas'd.
Ioue tooke his leaue, and parted from her sight,
Whose thoughts were ful of louers sweet delight,
And she ascended to her throne aboue,
To heare the griefes of the great Queene of loue.
But she was satisfide, and would no more
Rayle at her husband as she did before:
But forth she tript apace, because she stroue,
With her swift feet to ouertake great *Ioue,*
She skipt so nimbly as she went to looke him,
That at the palace doore she ouertooke him,
Which way was plaine and broade as they went out,

And now they could see no tumultuous rout.
Here *Venus* fearing, lest the loue of *Ioue*
Should make this mayd be plac'd in heauen aboue,
Because she thought this Nymph so wondrous bright,
That she would dazel her accustom'd light:
And fearing now she should not first be seene
Of all the glittering starres as shee had beene,
But that the wanton Nymph would eu'ry night
Be first that should salute eche mortal sight,
Began to tell great *Ioue*, she grieu'd to see
The heauen so full of his iniquity,
Complayning that eche strumpet now was grac'd,
And with immortall goddesses was plac'd,
Intreating him to place in heauen no more
Eche wanton strumpet and lasciuious whore.
Ioue mad with loue, harkned not what she sayd,
His thoughts were so intangled with the mayd,
But furiously he to his palace lept,
Being minded there till morning to haue slept:
For the next morne, as soone as *Phoebus* rayes
Should yet shine coole, by reason of the seas,
And ere the parting teares of *Thœtis* bed,
Should be quite shak't from off his glittring head,
Astrœa promis'd to attend great *Ioue*,
At his owne Palace in the heauen above,
And at that Palace she would set her hand
To what the loue-sick god should her command:
But to descend to earth she did deny,
She loath'd the sight of any mortall eye,
And for the compasse of the earthly round,
She would not set one foot vpon the ground.
Therefore *Ioue* meant to rise but with the sunne,
Yet thought it long vntill the night was done.
In the meane space *Venus* was drawne along

By her white Doues vnto the sweating throng
Of hammering Black-smithes, at the lofty hill
Of stately *Etna*, whose top burneth still:
(For at that burning mountaynes glittring top,
Her cripple husband *Vulcan* kept his shop)
To him she went, and so collogues that night
With the best straines of pleasures sweet delight,
That ere they parted, she made Vulcan sweare
By dreadfull *Stix*, an othe the gods do feare,
If *Ioue* would make the mortall mayd a starre,
Himselfe should frame his instruments of warre,
And tooke his othe by blacke *Cocitus* Lake,
He neuer more a thunder-bolt would make:
For *Venus* so this night his sences pleas'd,
That now he thought his former griefs were eas'd.
She with her hands the black-smiths body bound,
And with her Iu'ry armes she twyn'd him round,
And still the faire Queene with a prety grace,
Disperst her sweet breath o're his swarty face:
Her snowy armes so well she did display,
That *Vulcan* thought they melted as they lay.
Vntill the morne in this delight they lay:
Then vp they got, and hasted fast away
In the white Chariot of the Queene of loue,
Towards the Palace of great thundring *Ioue*,
Where they did see diuine *Astræa* stand,
To passe her word for what *Ioue* should command.
In limpt the Blacke-smith, after stept his Queene,
Whose light arrayment was of louely greene.
When they were in, *Vulcan* began to sweare
By othes that *Iupiter* himselfe doth feare,
If any whore in heauens bright vault were seene,
To dimme the shining of his beauteous Queene,
Each mortall man should the great gods disgrace,

And mocke almightie *Ioue* vnto his face,
And Giants should enforce bright heauen to fall,
Ere he would frame one thunderbolt at all.
Ioue did intreat him that he would forbeare.
The more he spoke, the more did *Vulcan* sweare.
Ioue heard his words, and 'gan to make his mone,
That mortall men would pluck him from his throne,
Or else he must incurre this plague, he said,
Quite to forgoe the pleasure of the mayd:
And once he thought, rather than lose her blisses,
Her heauenly sweets, her most delicious kisses,
Her soft embraces, and the amorous nights,
That he should often spend in her delights,
He would be quite thrown down by mortal hands,
From the blest place where his bright palace stands.
But afterwards hee saw with better sight,
He should be scorn'd by euery mortall wight,
If he should want his thunderbolts, to beate
Aspiring mortals from his glittering seate:
Therefore the god no more did woo or proue her,
But left to seeke her loue, though not to loue her.
Yet he forgot not that he woo'd the lasse,
But made her twise as beauteous as she was,
Because his wonted loue he needs would shew.
This haue I heard, but yet scarce thought it true.
And whether her cleare beautie was so bright,
That it could dazel the immortall sight
Of gods, and make them for her loue despaire,
I do not know; but sure the maid was faire.
Yet the faire Nymph was neuer seene resort
Vnto the sauage and the bloudy sport
Of chaste *Diana*, nor was euer wont
To bend a bow, nor euer did she hunt,
Nor did she euer striue with pretie cunning,

To ouergoe her fellow Nymphs in running:
For she was the faire water-Nymph alone,
That vnto chaste *Diana* was vnknowne.
It is reported, that her fellowes vs'd
To bid her (though the beauteous Nymph refus'd)
To take, or painted quiuers or a dart,
And put her lazy idlenesse apart.
Nor tooke she painted quiuers, nor a dart,
Nor put her lazy idlenesse apart,
But in her cristall fountaine oft she swimmes,
And oft she washes o're her snowy limmes:
Sometimes she com'b her soft discheuel'd hayre,
Which with a fillet tide she oft did weare:
But sometimes loose she did it hang behind,
When she was pleas'd to grace the Easterne wind:
For vp and downe it would her tresses hurle,
And as she went, it made her loose hayre curl:
Oft in the water did she looke her face,
And oft she vs'd to practise what quaint grace
Might well become her, and what comely feature
Might be best fitting so diuine a creature.
Her skinne was with a thinne vaile ouerthrowne,
Through which her naked beauty clearly shone.
She vs'd in this light rayment as she was,
To spread her body on the dewy grasse:
Sometimes by her owne fountaine as she walkes,
She nips the flowres from off the fertile stalkes,
And with a garland of the sweating vine,
Sometimes she doth her beauteous front in-twine:
But she was gathering flowres with her white hand,
When she beheld *Hermaphroditus* stand
By her cleare fountaine, wondring at the sight,
That there was any brooke could be so bright:
For this was the bright riuer where the boy

Did dye himselfe, that he could not enioy
Himselfe in pleasure, nor could taste the blisses
Of his owne melting and delicious kisses.
Here she did see him, and by *Venus* law,
She did desire to haue him as she saw:
But the fayre Nymph had neuer seene the place,
Where the boy was, nor his inchanting face,
But by an vncouth accident of loue
Betwixt great *Phoebus* and the sonne of *Ioue*,
Light -headed *Bacchus*: for vpon a day,
As the boy-god was keeping on his way,
Bearing his Vine leaues and his Iuie bands,
To *Naxos*, where his house and temple stands,
He saw the Nymph, and seeing, he did stay,
And threw his leaues and Iuie bands away,
Thinking at first she was of heauenly birth,
Some goddesse that did liue vpon the earth,
Virgin *Diana* that so liuely shone,
When she did court her sweet *Endimion*:
But he a god, at last did plainely see,
She had no marke of immortalitie.
Vnto the Nymph went the yong god of wine,
Whose head was chaf'd so with the bleeding vine,
That now, or feare or terrour had he none,
But 'gan to court her as she sate alone:
Fayrer then fayrest (thus began his speech)
Would but your radiant eye please to inrich
My eye with looking, or one glaunce to giue,
Whereby my other parts might feede and liue,
Or with one sight my sences to inspire,
Far liuelier then the stole *Promethean* fire;
Then I might liue, then by the sunny light
That should proceed from thy thrise-radiant sight,
I might suruiue to ages; but that missing,

(At that same word he would haue faine bin kissing)
I pine, fayre Nymph: O neuer let me dye
For one poore glaunce from thy translucent eye,
Farre more transparent then the clearest brooke.
The Nymph was taken with his golden hooke:
Yet she turn'd backe, and would haue tript away;
But *Bacchus* forc't the louely mayd to stay,
Asking her why she struggled to be gone,
Why such a Nymph should wish to be alone?
Heauen neuer made her faire, that she should vaunt
She kept all beautie, it would neuer graunt
She should be borne so beauteous from her mother,
But to reflect her beauty on another:
Then with a sweet kisse cast thy beames on mee,
And Ile reflect then backe againe on thee.
At Naxos stands my Temple and my Shrine,
Where I do presse the lusty swelling Vine,
There with green Iuie shall thy head be bound,
And with the red Grape be incircled round;
There shall *Silenus* sing vnto thy praise,
His drunken reeling songs and tickling layes.
Come hither, gentle Nymph. Here blusht the maid,
And faine she would haue gone, but yet she staid.
Bacchus perceiued he had o'ercome the lasse,
And downe he throwes her in the dewy grasse,
And kist the helplesse Nymph vpon the ground,
And would haue stray'd beyond that lawful bound.
This saw bright *Phœbus*: for his glittering eye
Sees all that lies below the starry skye;
And for an old affection that he bore
Vnto this louely Nymph long time before,
(For he would ofttimes in his circle stand,
To sport himselfe vpon her snowy hand)
He kept her from the sweets of *Bacchus* bed,

And 'gainst her will he sau'd her maiden-head.
Bacchus perceiuing this apace did hie
Vnto the Palace of swift *Mercury*:
But he did find him farre below his birth,
Drinking with theiues and catch-poles on the earth;
And they were drinking what they stole to day,
In consultation for to morrowes prey.
To him went youthful *Bacchus*, and begun
To shew his cause of griefe against the Sunne,
How he bereft him of his heauenly blisses,
His sweet delights, his Nectar-flowing kisses,
And other sweeter sweetes that he had wonne,
But for the malice of the bright-fac't Sunne,
Intreating *Mercury* by all the loue,
That had bene borne amongst the sonnes of *Ioue*,
Of which they two were part, to stand his friend,
Against the god that did him so offend:
The quaint-tongu'd issue of great *Atlas* race,
Swift *Mercury*, that with delightfull grace,
And pleasing accents of his fayned tongue,
Hath oft reform'd a rude vnciuill throng
Of mortals; that great messenger of *Ioue*,
And all the meaner gods that dwell aboue:
He whose acute wit was so quicke and sharpe
In the inuention of the crooked Harpe:
He that's so cunning with his iesting slights,
To steale from heauenly gods or earthly wights,
Bearing a great hate in his grieued brest,
Against that great commaunder of the West,
Bright-fac't *Apollo*: for vpon a day,
Yong *Mercury* did steale his beasts away:
Which the great god perceiuing, streight did shew
The pearcing arrowes and the fearefull bow
That kild great *Pithon*, & with that did threat him,

143

To bring his beast againe, or he would beat him.
Which *Mercury* perceiuing, vnespide,
Did closely steale his arrowes from his side.
For this olde grudge, he was the easlyer wonne
To helpe young *Bacchus* 'gainst the fierie Sunne.
And now the Sunne was in the middle way,
And had o'ercome the one halfe of the day,
Scorching so hot vpon the reeking sand,
That lies vpon the neere *Egyptian* land,
That the hot people burnt e'ne from their birth,
Do creepe againe into their mother earth,
When *Mercury* did take his powerfull wand,
His charming *Cadusæus* in his hand,
And a thick Beuer which he vs'd to weare,
When ought from *Ioue* he to the Sunne did beare,
That did protect him from the piercing light,
Which did proceed from *Phoebus* glittering sight.
Clad in these powerfull ornaments he flies,
With out-stretcht wings vp to the azure skies:
Where seeing *Phoebus* in his orient shrine,
He did so well reuenge the god of wine,
That whil'st the Sun wonders his Chariot reeles,
The craftie god had stole away his wheeles.
Which when he did perceiue, he downe did slide,
(Laying his glittering Coronet aside)
From the bright spangled firmament aboue,
To seeke the Nymph that *Bacchus* so did loue,
And found her looking in her watry glasse,
To see how cleare her radiant beauty was:
And, for he had but little time to stay,
Because he meant to finish out his day,
At the first sight he 'gan to make his mone,
Telling her how his fiery wheeles were gone;
Promising her, if she would but obtaine

The wheeles, that *Mercury* had stolne, againe,
That he might end his day, she should enioy
The heauenly sight of the most beauteous boy
That euer was. The Nymph was pleas'd with this,
Hoping to reape some vnaccustom'd blisse
By the sweet pleasure that she should enioy,
In the blest sight of such a melting boy.
Therefore at his request she did obtaine
The burning wheeles, that he had lost, againe:
Which when he had receiu'd, he left the land,
And brought them thither where his Coach did stand,
And there he set them on: for all this space,
The horses had not stirr'd from out their place.
Which when he saw, he wept and 'gan to say,
Would *Mercury* had stole my wheeles away,
When *Phaeton* my hare-brain'd issue tride,
What a laborious thing it was to guide
My burning chariot, then he might haue pleas'd me,
And of one fathers griefe he might haue eas'd me:
For then the Steeds would haue obayd his will,
Or else at least they would haue rested still.
When he had done, he tooke his whip of steele,
Whose bitter smart he made his horses feele:
For he did lash so hard, to end the day,
That he was quickly at the Westerne sea,
And there with *Thœtis* did he rest a space,
For he did neuer rest in any place
Before that time: but euer since his wheeles
Were stole away, his burning chariot reeles
Tow'rds the declining of the parting day:
Therefore he lights and mends them in the sea.
And though the poets fayne, that *Ioue* did make
A treble night for faire *Alcmena*'s sake,
That he might sleepe securely with his loue;

Yet sure the long night was vnknowne to Ioue:
But the Sunnes wheeles one day disordred more,
Were thrise as long amending as before.
Now was the Sunne inuiron'd with the Sea,
Cooling his watrie tresses as he lay,
And in dread *Neptunes* kingdome while he sleeps,
Faire *Thætis* clips him in the watry deeps,
The *Mayre-maids* and the *Tritons* of the West,
Strayning their voyces, to make *Titan* rest.
And while the blacke night with her pitchie hand,
Tooke iust possession of the swarfie land:
He spent the darkesome howres in this delight,
Giuing his power vp to the gladsome night:
For ne're before he was so truely blest,
To take an houre or one poore minutes rest.
But now the burning god this pleasure feeles,
By reason of his newly crazed wheeles,
There must he stay vntill lame *Vulcan* send
The fierie wheeles which he had tooke to mend.
Now al the night the Smith so hard had wrought,
That ere the Sunne could wake, his wheeles were brought.
Titan being pleas'd with rest, and not to rise,
And loth to open yet his slumbring eyes:
And yet perceiuing how the longing sight
Of mortals wayted for his glittring light,
He sent *Aurora* from him to the skie,
To giue a glimsing to each mortall eye.
Aurora much asham'd of that same place
That great *Apollos* light was wont to grace,
Finding no place to hide her shamefull head,
Paynted her chaste cheeks with a blushing red,
Which euer since remain'd vpon her face,
In token of her new receiu'd disgrace:
Therefore she not so white as she had beene,

Lothing of eu'ry mortall to be seene,
No sooner can the rosie fingred morne
Kisse eu'ry flowre that by her dew is borne,
But from her golden window she doth peepe,
When the most part of earthly creatures sleepe.
By this, bright *Titan* opened had his eyes,
And 'gan to ierke his horses through the skies,
And taking in his hand his fierie whip,
He made *AEous* and swift *AEthon* skip
So fast, that straight he dazled had the sight
Of faire *Aurora*, glad to see his light.
And now the Sunne in all his fierie haste,
Did call to mind his promise lately past,
And all the vowes and othes that he did passe
Vnto faire *Salmacis*, the beauteous lasse:
For he had promis'd her she should enioy
So louely faire, and such a well shapt boy,
As ne're before his owne all-seeing eye
Saw from his bright seate in the starry skye:
Remembring this, he sent the boy that way,
Where the cleare fountain of the fayre Nymph lay.
There was he come to seeke some pleasing brooke.
No sooner came he, but the Nymph was strooke:
And though she hasted to imbrace the boy,
Yet did the Nymph awhile deferre her ioy,
Till she had bound vp her loose flagging haire,
And ordred well the garments she did weare,
Fayning her count'nance with a louers care,
And did deserue to be accounted fayre.
And thus much spake she while the boy abode:
O boy, most worthy to be thought a god,
Thou mayst inhabit in the glorious place
Of gods, or maist proceed from human race:
Thou mayst be *Cupid*, or the god of wine,

That lately woo'd me with the swelling vine:
But whosoe're thou art, O happy he,
That was so blest, to be a sire to thee;
Thy happy mother is most blest of many,
Blessed thy sisters, if her wombe bare any,
Both fortunate, and O thrise happy shee,
Whose too much blessed breasts gaue suck to thee:
If any wife with thy sweet bed be blest,
O, she is farre more happy then the rest;
If thou hast any, let my sport be sto'ne,
Or else let me be she, if thou haue none.
Here did she pause a while, and then she sayd,
Be not obdurate to a silly mayd.
A flinty heart within a smowy brest,
Is like base mold lockt in a golden chest:
They say the eye's the Index of the heart,
And shewes th'affection of each inward part:
There loue playes liuely, there the little god
Hath a cleare cristall Palace of abode.
O barre him not from playing in thy heart,
That sports himselfe vpon eche outward part.
Thus much she spake, & then her tongue was husht.
At her loose speach *Hermaphroditus* blusht:
He knew not what loue was, yet loue did shame him,
Making him blush, and yet his blush became him:
Then might a man his shamefast colour see,
Like the ripe apple on the sunny tree,
Or Iuory dide o're with a pleasing red,
Or like the pale Moone being shadowed.
By this, the Nymph recouer'd had her tongue,
That to her thinking lay in silence long,
And sayd, Thy cheeke is milde, O be thou so,
Thy cheeke, saith I, then do not answere no,
Thy cheeke doth shame, then doe thou shame, she sayd,

It is a mans shame to deny a mayd.
Thou look'st to sport with *Venus* in her towre,
And be belou'd of euery heauenly powre.
Men are but mortals, so are women too,
Why should your thoughts aspire more than ours doo?
For sure they doe aspire: Else could a youth,
Whose count'nance is so full of spotlesse truth,
Be so relentlesse to a virgins tongue?
Let me be woo'd by thee but halfe so long,
With halfe those tearmes doe but my loue require,
And I will easly graunt thee thy desire.
Ages are bad, when men become so slow,
That poore vnskillful mayds are forc't to woo.
Her radiant beauty and her subtill arte
S deepely strooke *Hermaphroditus* heart,
That she had wonne his loue, but that the light
Of her translucent eyes did shine too bright:
For long he look'd vpon the louely mayd,
And at the last *Hermaphroditus* sayd,
How should I loue thee, when I doe espie
A farre more beauteous Nymph hid in thy eye?
When thou doost loue, let not that Nymph be nie thee;
Nor when thou woo'st, let not that Nymph be by thee:
Or quite obscure her from thy louers face,
Or hide her beauty in a darker place.
By this, the Nymph perceiu'd he did espie
None but himselfe reflected in her eye,
And, for himselfe no more she meant to shew him,
She shut her eyes & blind-fold thus did woo him:
Fayre boy, thinke not thy beauty can dispence
With any payne due to a bad offence;
Remember how the gods punisht that boy
That scorn'd to let a beauteous Nymph enioy
Her long wisht pleasure, for the peeuish elfe,

Lou'd of all other, needs would loue himselfe.
So mayst thou loue, perhaps thou mayst be blest;
By graunting to a lucklesse Nymphs request:
Then rest awhile with me amid these weeds.
The Sunne that sees all, sees not louers deeds;
Phoebus is blind when loue-sports are begun,
And neuer sees vntill their sports be done:
Beleeue me, boy, thy blood is very stayd,
That art so loth to kisse a youthfull mayd.
Wert thou a mayd, and I a man, Ile show thee,
With what a manly boldnesse I could woo thee,
Fayrer then loues Queene, thus I would begin,
Might not my ouer-boldnesse be a sinne,
I would intreat this fauor, if I could,
Thy rosiat cheeke a little to behold:
Then would I beg a touch, and then a kisse,
And then a lower, yet a higher blisse:
Then would I aske what *Ioue* and *Læda* did,
When like a Swan the craftie god was hid?
What came he for? why did he there abide?
Surely I thinke hee did not come to chide:
He came to see her face, to talke, and chat,
To touch, to kisse: came he for nought but that?
Yea, something else: what was it he would haue?
That which all men of maydens ought to craue.
This sayd, her eye-lids wide she did display:
But in this space the boy was runne away:
The wanton speeches of the louely lasse
Forc't him for shame to hide him in the grasse.
When she perceiu'd she could not see him neere her,
When she had cal'd and yet he could not heare her,
Look how when *Autumne* comes, a little space
Paleth the red blush of the Summers face,
Tearing the leaues the Summers couering,

Three months in weauing by the curious spring,
Making the grasse his greene locks go to wracke,
Tearing each ornament from off his backe;
So did she spoyle the garments she did weare,
Tearing whole ounces of her golden hayre:
She thus deluded of her longed blisse,
With much adoo at last she vttred this:
Why wert thou bashfull, boy? Thou hast no part
Shewes thee to be of such a female heart.
His eye is gray, so is the mornings eye,
That blusheth alwayes when the day is nye.
Then his gray eye's the cause: that cannot be:
The gray-ey'd morne is farre more bold then he:
For with a gentle dew from heauens bright towre,
It gets the mayden-head of eu'ry flowre.
I would to God, he were the rosiat morne,
And I a flowre from out the earth new-borne?
His face was smooth; *Narcissus* face was so,
And he was carelesse of a sad Nymphs woe.
Then that's the cause; and yet that cannot be:
Youthfull *Narcissus* was more bold then he,
Because he dide for loue, though of his shade:
This boy nor loues himselfe, nor yet a mayd.
Besides, his glorious eye is wondrous bright;
So is the fierie and all-seeing light
Of *Phœbus*, who at eu'ry mornings birth
Blusheth for shame vpon the sullen earth.
Then that's the cause; and yet that cannot be:
The fierie Sunne is farre more bold then he;
He nightly kisseth *Thœtis* in the sea:
All know the story of *Leucothoe*.
His cheeke is red: so is the fragrant Rose,
Whose ruddie cheeke with ouer-blushing gloes:
Then that's the cause; and yet that cannot bee:

Eche blushing Rose is farre more bold then he,
Whose boldnesse may be plainely seene in this,
The ruddy Rose is not asham'd to kisse;
For alwayes when the day is new begun,
The spreading Rose will kisse the morning Sun.
This sayd, hid in the grasse she did espie him,
And stumbling with her will, she fel down by him,
And with her wanton talke, because he woo'd not,
Beg'd that, which he poore nouice vnderstood not:
And, for she could not get a greater blisse,
She did intreate a least a sisters kisse;
But still the more she did the boy beseech,
The more he powted at her wanton speech.
At last the Nymph began to touch his skin,
Whiter then mountaine snow hath euer bin,
And did in purenesse that cleare spring surpasse,
Wherein *Acteon* saw th'Arcadian lasse.
Thus did she dally long, till at the last,
In her moyst palme she lockt his white hand fast:
Then in her hand his wrest she 'gan to close,
When through his pulses strait the warm bloud gloes,
Whose youthfull musike fanning *Cupids* fire,
In her warme brest kindled a fresh desire.
Then did she lift her hand vnto his brest,
A part as white and youthfull as the rest,
Where, as his flowry breath still comes and goes,
She felt his gentle heart pant through his clothes.
At last she tooke her hand from off that part,
And sayd, It panted like anothers heart.
Why should it be more feeble, and lesse bold?
Why should the bloud about it be more cold?
Nay sure, that yeelds, onely thy tongue denyes,
And the true fancy of thy heart belyes.
Then did she lift her hand vnto his chin,

And prays'd the prety dimpling of his skin:
But straight his chin she 'gan to ouerslip,
When she beheld the rednesse of his lip;
And sayd, thy lips are soft, presse them to mine,
And thou shalt see they are as soft as thine.
Then would she faine haue gone vnto his eye,
But still his ruddy lip standing so nie,
Drew her hand backe, therefore his eye she mist,
'Ginning to claspe his neck, and would haue kist;
But then the boy did struggle to be gone,
Vowing to leaue her and that place alone.
But then bright *Salmacis* began to feare,
And sayd, Fayre stranger, I wil leaue thee here
Amid these pleasant places all alone.
So turning back, she fayned to be gone;
But from his sight she had no power to passe,
Therefore she turn'd and hid her in the grasse,
When to the ground bending her snow-white knee,
The glad earth gaue new coates to euery tree.
He then supposing he was all alone,
(Like a young boy that is espy'd of none)
Runnes here, and there, then on the bankes doth looke,
Then on the cristall current of the brooke,
Then with his foote he toucht the siluer streames,
Whose drowsy waues made musike in their dreames,
And, for he was not wholy in, did weepe,
Talking alowd and babbling in their sleepe:
Whose pleasant coolnesse when the boy did feele,
He thrust his foote downe lower to the heele:
O'ercome with whose sweet noyse, he did begin
To strip his soft clothes from his tender skin,
When strait the scorching Sun wept teares of brine,
Because he durst not touch him with his shine,
For feare of spoyling that same Iu'ry skin,

153

Whose whitenesse he so much delighted in;
And then the Moone, mother of mortall ease,
Would fayne haue come from the *Antipodes*,
To haue beheld him naked as he stood,
Ready to leape into the siluer flood;
But might not: for the lawes of heauen deny,
To shew mens secrets to a womans eye:
And therefore was her sad and gloomy light
Confin'd vnto the secret-keeping night.
When beauteous *Salmacis* awhile had gaz'd
Vpon his naked corps, she stood amaz'd,
And both her sparkling eyes burnt in her face,
Like the bright Sunne reflected in a glasse:
Scarce can she stay from running to the boy,
Scarce can she now deferre her hoped ioy;
So fast her youthfull bloud playes in her vaynes,
That almost mad, she scarce herselfe contaynes.
When young *Hermaphroditus* as he stands,
Clapping his white side with his hollow hands,
Leapt liuely from the land, whereon he stood,
Into the mayne part of the cristall flood.
Like Iu'ry then his snowy body was,
Or a white Lilly in a christall glasse.
Then rose the water Nymph from where she lay,
As hauing wonne the glory of the day,
And her light garments cast from off her skin,
Hee's mine, she cry'd, and so leapt spritely in.
The flattering Iuy who did euer see
Inclaspe the huge trunke of an aged tree,
Let him behold the young boy as he stands,
Inclaspt in wanton *Salmacis*'s hands,
Betwixt those Iu'ry armes she lockt him fast,
Striuing to get away, till at the last,
Fondling, she sayd, why striu'st thou to be gone?

154

Why shouldst thou so desire to be alone?
Thy cheeke is neuer fayre, when none is by:
For what is red and white, but to the eye:
And for that cause the heauens are darker at night,
Because all creatures close their weary sight;
For there's no mortall can so earely rise,
But still the morning waytes vpon his eyes.
The earely-rising and soone-singing Larke
Can neuer chaunt her sweete notes in the darke,
For sleepe she ne're so little or so long,
Yet still the morning will attend her song.
All creatures that beneath bright *Cinthia* be,
Haue appetite vnto society;
The ouerflowing waues would haue a bound
Within the confines of the spacious ground,
And all their shady currents would be plaste
In hollow of the solitary vaste,
But what they lothe to let their soft streames sing,
Where non can heare their gentle murmuring.
Yet still the boy regardlesse what she sayd,
Struggled apace to ouerswimme the mayd.
Which when the Nymph perceiu'd she 'gan to say,
Struggle thou mayst, but neuer get away.
So graunt, iust gods, that neuer day may see
The separation twixt this boy and mee.
The gods did heare her pray'r and feele her woe;
And in one body they began to grow.
She felt his youthfull bloud in euery vaine;
And he felt hers warme his colde brest againe.
And euer since was womans loue so blest,
That it will draw bloud from the strongerst brest.
Nor man nor mayd now could they be esteem'd:
Neither, and either, might they well be deem'd,
When the young boy *Hermaphroditus* sayd,

With the set voyce of neither man nor mayd,
Swift *Mercury*, the author of my life,
And thou my mother *Vulcans* louely wife,
Let your poore offsprings latest breath be blest,
In but obtayning this his last request,
Grant that whoe're heated by *Phoebus* beames,
Shall come to coole him in these siluer streames,
May neuermore a manly shape retaine,
But halfe a virgine may returne againe.
His parents hark'ned to his last request,
And with that great power they the fountaine blest.
And since that time who in that fountaine swimmes,
A mayden smoothnesse seyzeth half his limmes.

FINIS

.

Also from Benediction Books ...

Wandering Between Two Worlds: Essays on Faith and Art
Anita Mathias
Benediction Books, 2007
152 pages
ISBN: 0955373700

Available from www.amazon.com, www.amazon.co.uk
www.wanderingbetweentwoworlds.com

In these wide-ranging lyrical essays, Anita Mathias writes, in lush, lovely prose, of her naughty Catholic childhood in Jamshedpur, India; her large, eccentric family in Mangalore, a sea-coast town converted by the Portuguese in the sixteenth century; her rebellion and atheism as a teenager in her Himalayan boarding school, run by German missionary nuns, St. Mary's Convent, Nainital; and her abrupt religious conversion after which she entered Mother Teresa's convent in Calcutta as a novice. Later rich, elegant essays explore the dualities of her life as a writer, mother, and Christian in the United States-- Domesticity and Art, Writing and Prayer, and the experience of being "an alien and stranger" as an immigrant in America, sensing the need for roots.

About the Author

Anita Mathias was born in India, has a B.A. and M.A. in English from Somerville College, Oxford University and an M.A. in Creative Writing from the Ohio State University. Her essays have been published in The Washington Post, The London Magazine, The Virginia Quarterly Review, Commonweal, Notre Dame Magazine, America, The Christian Century, Religion Online, The Southwest Review, Contemporary Literary Criticism, New Letters, The Journal, and two of HarperSanFrancisco's The Best Spiritual Writing anthologies. Her non-fiction has won fellowships from The National Endowment for the Arts; The Minnesota State Arts Board; The Jerome Foundation, The Vermont Studio Center; The Virginia Centre for the Creative Arts, and the First Prize for the Best General Interest Article from the Catholic Press Association of the United States and Canada. Anita has taught Creative Writing at the College of William and Mary, and now lives and writes in Oxford, England.

"Yesterday's Treasures for Today's Readers"
Titles by Benediction Classics available from Amazon.co.uk

Religio Medici, Hydriotaphia, Letter to a Friend, Thomas Browne

Pseudodoxia Epidemica: Or, Enquiries into Commonly Presumed Truths, Thomas Browne

Urne Buriall and The Garden of Cyrus, Thomas Browne

The Maid's Tragedy, Beaumont and Fletcher

The Custom of the Country, Beaumont and Fletcher

Philaster Or Love Lies a Bleeding, Beaumont and Fletcher

A Treatise of Fishing with an Angle,   Dame Juliana Berners.

Pamphilia to Amphilanthus, Lady Mary Wroth

The Compleat Angler, Izaak Walton

The Magnetic Lady, Ben Jonson

Every Man Out of His Humour, Ben Jonson

The Masque of Blacknesse. The Masque of Beauty,. Ben Jonson

The Life of St. Thomas More, William Roper

Pendennis, William Makepeace Thackeray

Salmacis and Hermaphroditus attributed to Francis Beaumont

Friar Bacon and Friar Bungay Robert Greene

Holy Wisdom, Augustine Baker

The Jew of Malta and the Massacre at Paris, Christopher Marlowe

Tamburlaine the Great, Parts 1 & 2 AND Massacre at Paris, Christopher Marlowe

All Ovids Elegies, Lucans First Booke, Dido Queene of Carthage, Hero and Leander, Christopher Marlowe

The Titan, Theodore Dreiser

Scapegoats of the Empire: The true story of the Bushveldt Carbineers, George Witton

All Hallows' Eve, Charles Williams

The Place of The Lion, Charles Williams

The Greater Trumps, Charles Williams

My Apprenticeship: Volumes I and II, Beatrice Webb

Last and First Men / Star Maker, Olaf Stapledon

Last and First Men, Olaf Stapledon

Darkness and the Light, Olaf Stapledon

The Worst Journey in the World, Apsley Cherry-Garrard

The Schoole of Abuse, Containing a Pleasaunt Invective Against Poets, Pipers, Plaiers, Iesters and Such Like Catepillers of the Commonwelth, Stephen Gosson

Russia in the Shadows, H. G. Wells

Wild Swans at Coole, W. B. Yeats

A hundreth good pointes of husbandrie, Thomas Tusser

The Collected Works of Nathanael West: "The Day of the Locust", "The Dream Life of Balso Snell", "Miss Lonelyhearts", "A Cool Million", Nathanael West

Miss Lonelyhearts & The Day of the Locust, Nathaniel West

The Worst Journey in the World, Apsley Cherry-Garrard

Scott's Last Expedition, V1, R. F. Scott

The Dream of Gerontius, John Henry Newman

The Brother of Daphne, Dornford Yates

The Downfall of Robert Earl of Huntington, Anthony Munday

Clayhanger, Arnold Bennett

The Regent, A Five Towns Story Of Adventure In London , Arnold Bennett

The Card, A Story Of Adventure In The Five Towns , Arnold Bennett

South: The Story of Shackleton's Last Expedition 1914-1917, Sir Ernest Shackketon

Greene's Groatsworth of Wit: Bought With a Million of Repentance, Robert Greene

Beau Sabreur, Percival Christopher Wren

Christ Legends: And Other Stories, Selma Lagerlof; (trans. Velma Swanston Howard)

Chamber Music, James Joyce

Blurt, Master Constable, Thomas Middleton, Thomas Dekker

Since Yesterday, Frederick Lewis Allen

The Scholemaster: Or, Plaine and Perfite Way of Teachyng Children the Latin Tong, Roger Ascham

The Wonderful Year, 1603, Thomas Dekker

Waverley, Sir Walter Scott

Guy Mannering, Sir Walter Scott

Old Mortality, Sir Walter Scott

The Knight of Malta, John Fletcher

The Double Marriage, John Fletcher and Philip Massinger

Space Prison, Tom Godwin

The Home of the Blizzard Being the Story of the Australasian Antarctic Expedition, 1911-1914, Douglas Mawson

Wild-goose Chase , John Fletcher

If You Know Not Me, You Know Nobody. Part I and Part II, Thomas Heywood

The Ragged Trousered Philanthropists, Robert Tressell

The Island of Sheep, John Buchan

Eyes of the Woods, Joseph Altsheler

The Club of Queer Trades, G. K. Chesterton

The Financier, Theodore Dreiser

Something of Myself, Rudyard Kipling

Law of Freedom in a Platform, or True Magistracy Restored, Gerrard Winstanley

Damon and Pithias, Richard Edwards

Dido Queen of Carthage: And, The Massacre at Paris, Christopher Marlowe

Cocoa and Chocolate: Their History from Plantation to Consumer, Arthur Knapp

Lady of Pleasure, James Shirley

The South Pole: An account of the Norwegian Antarctic expedition in the "Fram," 1910-12. Volume 1 and Volume 2, Roald Amundsen

A Yorkshire Tragedy, Thomas Middleton (attrib.)

The Tragedy of Soliman and Perseda, Thomas Kyd

The Rape of Lucrece. Thomas Heywood

Myths and Legends of Ancient Greece and Rome, E. M. Berens

In the Forbidden Land, Henry Savage Arnold Landor

Illustrated History of Furniture: From the Earliest to the Present Time, Frederick Litchfield

A Narrative of Some of the Lord's Dealings with George Müller Written by Himself (Parts I-IV, 1805-1856), George Müller

The Towneley Cycle Of The Mystery Plays (Or The Wakefield Cycle): Thirty-Two Pageants, Anonymous

The Insatiate Countesse, John Marston.

Spontaneous Activity in Education, Maria Montessori.

On the Art of Writing, Sir Arthur Quiller-Couch

The Well of the Saints, J. M. Synge

Bacon's Advancement Of Learning And The New Atlantis, Francis Bacon.

Catholic Tales And Christian Songs, Dorothy Sayers.

Two Little Savages: Being the Adventures of Two Boys who Lived as Indians and What they Learned, Ernest Thompson Seton

The Sadness of Christ, Thomas More

The Family of Love, Thomas Middleton

The Passing of the Aborigines: A Lifetime Spent Among the Natives of Australia, Daisy Bates

The Children, Edith Wharton

and many others…

Lightning Source UK Ltd.
Milton Keynes UK
UKHW011602050922
408362UK00002B/283